Texas Gulag

The Chain Gang Years
1875-1925

Gary Brown

Republic of Texas Press
Plano, Texas

Library of Congress Cataloging-in-Publication Data

Brown, Gary., 1945-
    Texas Gulag : the chain gang years, 1875-1925 / Gary Brown.
        p.   cm.
    Includes bibliographical references and index.
    ISBN 1-55622-931-3
    1. Prisoners—Texas—Biography.   2. Imprisonment—Texas—Case studies.
    3. Punishment—Texas—Case studies.   4. Torture—Texas—Case studies.
    5. Prisons—Texas—History.   I. Title.

    HV9475.T4 B76 2002
    365'.65—dc21   2001058926
                                                             CIP

Republic of Texas Press is an imprint of Wordware Publishing, Inc.
No part of this book may be reproduced in any form or by
any means without permission in writing from
Wordware Publishing, Inc.

Printed in the United States of America

ISBN 1-55622-931-3
10 9 8 7 6 5 4 3 2 1
0201

All inquiries for volume purchases of this book should be addressed to
Wordware Publishing, Inc., at 2320 Los Rios Boulevard, Plano, Texas 75074.
Telephone inquiries may be made by calling:

(972) 423-0090

Contents

Contents

Preface

In 2000, less than a year after my retirement from the Texas Department of Criminal Justice, I was visiting an antique shop in Fowler, Colorado, and came upon a small and very old brochure titled *Seven Years in Texas Prisons*. After twenty-three years working in those prisons, I hardly wanted to read about them, but the age and appearance of the pamphlet intrigued me.

I purchased it, packed it away, and forgot about it until several weeks after I'd returned home. When I finally sat down and read it, I was fascinated. It was a tiny 4½-by-5½-inch booklet only twenty-four pages in length, but in those pages, a former Texas prison convict named Beecher Deason wrote eloquently of the conditions inside Texas prisons in the early 1920s.

He wrote of the prison farms in the years immediately after the abolition of the convict lease system, and what he described—the food, housing, punishments, building tenders, and brutality—portrayed a prison system I had heard about but never seen during my career.

Curious if any other convicts had written similar accounts of time in the early years of Texas prisons, I searched without success until I discovered a collection at the Center for American History at the University of Texas at Austin. They had several such narratives, and they dated back into the 1880s.

As I examined them, I found stories and accounts of serving time in Texas during the convict lease system when prisoners were leased out to private individuals and organizations to work in sawmills, on cotton plantations, and at railroad construction sites.

The pre-1900 accounts were particularly damning in their portrayal of brutality, and my first reaction was to dismiss them as attempts to "get back" at the prison system that had incarcerated these men.

Then, also at the Center for American History, I came upon a massive state report titled *Report of the Penitentiary Investigating Committee including All Exhibits and Testimony Taken by the Committee, Published by Order of the House of Representatives, August 1910*. This report was an "official" state document issued by the legislature, and in it I discovered almost all of the allegations in the various narratives by ex-prisoners had been found to be true.

The tiny brochure I had purchased in a Colorado antique shop led to my collecting prison narratives dating from 1875 to 1925—a span of fifty years that can easily be classified as the most violent, brutal, and inhumane period of Texas correctional history.

The "kept" and the "keepers" have never seen eye-to-eye in the over 150 years of Texas prison history. And many times during that period, individuals, organizations, and state agencies have asked the question, "Who guards the guards?"

But it is the inmates who historically bear the greatest grudge against the system that incarcerates them.

During the late 1800s and the first decades of the following century, convicts unfortunate enough to be sentenced to Texas prisons and fortunate enough to survive to be paroled or discharged had few venues available to them in which to vent their anger and frustration at a system continuously in turmoil over charges of brutality and corruption.

The years leading up to the Great Depression were an extended period in which the Texas prison system was a state agency shrouded in secrecy. It would be many decades before convicts would have access to high profile media-oriented attorneys, sensational headline-seeking television investigative reporters, in-depth newspaper reports, and a federal judicial system that involved itself in Texas prison affairs from afar and without a clue as to how to solve the problems.

In essence, ex-convicts during the period of 1875 through 1925 had only one option available should they choose to try to inform the public about the brutality and corruption they claimed to have witnessed from inside Texas prisons.

They could write their memoirs.

And they did so, telling of the daily work quotas of seven tons of coal, three hundred pounds of cotton, or one and one-half cords of wood. They told of eating spoiled hog meat and sleeping on mattresses filled with bugs and filthy from sweat, blood, and dirt. They told of various punishments they endured, especially the hated "bat" that would be used in Texas prisons until the 1940s.

Texas Gulag: The Chain Gang Years 1875 - 1925 is a collection of those stories. Interspersed are detailed descriptions, many of which were taken directly from the 1910 *Report of the Penitentiary Investigating Committee*.

The inmates who wrote these accounts were obviously among the better-educated convicts of that period. But they, too, reflected the attitudes and prejudices of that fifty-year span. And they were criminals with an "axe to grind."

The convict lease system in Texas, as in most other southern states, was a product of post-Reconstruction, however as early as 1867 Texas was leasing prisoners to railroads. Administrative problems resulted in the termination of those leases, and in 1877 Texas leased out the entire prison system—buildings, administration, and convicts—to private interests. One of the results of this was the construction of a second prison unit at Rusk.

By 1883 Texas had resumed control of the prison system but continued to lease out prisoners to work in cotton fields, sawmills, coal mines, and on railroads while purchasing land and establishing its own farm system.

It is at this time most of the narratives in *Texas Gulag* took place. The sadistic and inhumane conditions of the work camps, alleged by the convicts and documented by the legislature in the 1910 report, led to pressure from the public to abolish the convict lease system completely. After the publication of the legislative report, the governor called a special session of the legislature and laws were enacted to end the program of leasing convicts to private interests in Texas. By 1912 all leases had been terminated and Texas convicts were exclusively under the control of the state.

Texas was somewhat unusual in that chain gangs were not used for road construction as in other southern states, and therefore these stories don't fit the typical stereotype of road gangs. Instead, Texas chain gangs tended to work in isolated areas far from the eyes of the public and even prison officials—in lumber camps, underground mines, and on rural farms and plantations.

After the Civil War, the Thirteenth Amendment was intended to end slavery and "involuntary servitude." After Reconstruction, "Black Codes" circumvented the integration of former slaves into society, and the "convict lease system" sent many former slaves back into their previous servitude status throughout the American South.

But Texas also differs from the other southern states in that only about half of Texas inmates leased out during this period were black; states from the "deep South" often reported up to ninety percent of their leased convicts being Negroes. In Texas, black inmates were usually leased to farming operations—working fields, picking cotton, and cutting sugarcane. White and Mexican inmates were sent to the lumber camps, coal mines, and railroads.

The terrible conditions and brutal treatment appear to have been system-wide and color-blind. The 1910 report would also document shocking treatment of female convicts in Texas during this era.

Those who wrote personal accounts of their imprisonment during this period tended to be white male ex-convicts. Because of this, *Texas Gulag* does not describe the convict lease period from the perspective of black or female inmates.

In 1984 Albert Race Sample wrote of his experiences as a black inmate on the infamous Retrieve unit during the 1950s in his book *Racehoss, Big Emma's Boy*. His well-written account gives an excellent description of the conditions in the Retrieve prison fields, but this occurred some four decades after the abolition of the lease system and is not included here.

Likewise the voices of female convicts are missing in these narratives. Very little information about their experiences from 1875 to 1925 is available. The 1910 *Report of the Penitentiary Investigating Committee* does contain several pages of interviews with the women imprisoned at the Eastham farm, and some of the allegations of the women and the conclusions of the committee are included in *Texas Gulag*.

During the 1980s I often felt, as a state prison employee, that I was witnessing the complete reformation of a state agency during the court-ordered reforms of that decade.

After reading the narratives of these men a century earlier, however, I realize that the Texas prison system has been in a continuous state of change since its inception after Texas joined the Union. Sadly, what current Texas prison officials don't realize—and I also missed it—is that the prison reform years of the 1930s make the current problems seem almost trivial.

Men like Lee Simmons, Albert Moore, and Bud Russell took an antiquated, post-lease prison system in total turmoil and mismanagement and forced it into the twentieth century.

The process was painful, and today's Texas Department of Criminal Justice does not even remember their names, much less what they endured, overcame, and established.

And as for the convicts who served time during that tumultuous period of 1875 to 1925, had they not written their personal narratives, they too would also probably be forgotten.

But they did write them, and thanks to Beecher Deason and *Seven Years in Texas Prisons*, here are their stories. Deason's introduction sets an appropriate stage:

> *Did you ever see the Devil? Have you ever been in Hell? Did you ever have an angel pay a visit to your cell in solitary confinement where men are seldom fed?*
>
> *I've seen it all in reality in the land of the living dead.*

Acknowledgments

The Brazoria County Historical Museum, in Angleton, may well be one of the best-organized "small" museums in the state, and the museum library has a tremendous collection of Brazoria County, Gulf Coast, and Texas historical materials. Ms. Jamie Murray, the Information Services Coordinator, has been of invaluable assistance in my various projects including tracing the histories of the various prison units located in that region.

The staff of the Texas Prison Museum has also been extremely helpful in explaining and providing information regarding the history of the Texas prison system. Located in an old bank building on the courthouse square in Huntsville, Texas, the museum and its mostly volunteer staff take what could be a grisly and morbid subject and portray the history of Texas prisons in a dignified, educational, and informative manner. Scheduled to move into a new permanent location in Huntsville in the future, the museum will be able to provide even more extensive and detailed information about the Texas prison system.

One of the chapters in my collection of stories about Texas prisoners, *Singin' a Lonesome Song,* involved Bud Russell—the transfer agent for the prison system during the first half of the 1900s. His great-grandson, Robert H. Russell Jr., contacted me after publication and for the past year, we have corresponded frequently. Robert has archived information and photographs relating to his relative and in the process, has become an expert on the early history of the Texas prison system. Some of his personal photographs of Bud Russell, on loan to the Texas

Prison Museum, were used as illustrations in *Singin' a Lonesome Song*, and he has been very generous in sharing with me stories and details of Bud Russell's career and the prison system—including some of the photographs used in *Texas Gulag*—from the early 1900s until 1944.

Chapter One

(1895-1909)

Fourteen Years in Hell

The Texas Prison Memoir of John Shotwell

We were fed on spoiled hog-head, stale corn bread and coffee made of burned corn bread crust. I have known men at this farm to put lime in their eyes and go blind, in order that they might be sent back to Rusk and have a chance to live through their sentence. One particularly severe winter they did not furnish half of us with shoes. We were occupied in wood cutting, and one night there came a cold spell and a fall of snow. I said to the captain next morning "I can't go out to cut wood today. I'm bare-footed." "That don't make a d—n bit of difference," he answered. "You're sent here to cut wood, and cut wood you will."

For fourteen years, John Shotwell experienced every type of convict lease camp the state of Texas sponsored. At various times he worked at the dreaded wood camp near Alto, the cotton plantations near Cameron, the deadly coal mines at Calvert, and finally, inside the Rusk prison itself. For fourteen years, spanning three sentences, he was leased out from 1895 through 1909.

From 1895 to 1909, John Shotwell was sentenced to almost every form of hell the Texas prison could devise: sawmill camps, the Calvert coal mines, picking cotton on the plantations, and finally inside Rusk prison. He later wrote his memoirs, which included this photo of himself. Shotwell, John, *A Victim of Revenge or Fourteen Years in Hell* (San Antonio: E.J. Jackson Co., 1909)

Sometime after his final discharge he published a compelling narrative of those experiences in which he described in detail the despair of being leased out to saw and chop wood, pick cotton, and shovel coal for profit-minded private companies who viewed inmates as temporary expendable assets.

The title of his prison memoir, *A Victim of Revenge or Fourteen Years in Hell*, suggests an indictment of the system he so detested but also suggests he felt himself the helpless victim of a corrupt and vindictive state political judicial system.

His legal problems began when he was a teenager trying to impress a young girl in Mount Pleasant, Texas, and ended when he finally left Texas prisons as a man "broken physically and emotionally."

Shotwell admits to forging checks at Mount Pleasant, a charge for which he received a harsh six-year prison sentence. Local officials apparently wanted to make an example of him by pursuing and obtaining a prison sentence for a first-time offense that usually resulted in probation and restitution.

However, they also obviously wanted to assure he never returned to their community.

Some of the forged checks that Shotwell passed around were cashed in neighboring counties, and after completion of his six-year sentence, he found himself immediately charged in one of those counties and resentenced to another six years. Upon completion of that second sentence, a third county filed charges on him and he was sentenced to yet a third prison term—all basically for one act of forging checks.

The title of his narrative, *A Victim of Revenge or Fourteen Years in Hell*, therefore not only suggests the brutality of the prison system but also suggests he considered himself the target of petty, politically ambitious prosecutors.

Shotwell's narrative is, in his words, not only an attempt to expose the corruption and brutality of the state prison lease system but also to steer young readers away from any thoughts of following his example. Much of his warning to younger readers is detailed through his frustration of trying to later live in society as an ex-convict.

He begins *A Victim of Revenge or Fourteen Years in Hell* with a warning to readers of the terrible effects incarceration had on ex-convicts in Texas society in the early 1900s. The first paragraph creates a stark image of former state prisoners:

> Only those who have been through it all themselves and into whose minds is scared [*sic*] its misery, can account for the strange and shapeless horror, the shuddering, nameless dread that haunts the sleeping and waking moments of the Texas ex-convict. Only these can account why he has acquired a dog-like submissiveness; why he has the aspect of a whipped cur; why he starts at every sound, ready to run or cringe; why he is broken in spirit, with vitality and self-control reduced to the minimum. Not until you have lived in

rotting rags, eating what a dog would almost spurn, slaved beneath the goad of cruel guards, been cursed at in your misery, and mocked at in your despair, until spirit and body alike are broken and cowed can you know what it means to be a convict on a Texas farm.

Unlike many other narratives of the lease period, Shotwell does not attribute his problems to poverty or family. Although he describes his early years as a period in which his family struggled with poverty, he also states that he came from a loving and nurturing Christian family.

Born in North Carolina on May 17, 1873, he recalled moving with his family to Farmersville, Texas, as a small child and growing up on the family farm. Much of his childhood was spent working in the cotton fields, hard work that offered little promise to a young man.

Despite the warm feelings he professed for his family, he ran away from home while a teenager, probably trying to escape those cotton fields, and eventually found himself at Mount Pleasant, where he claims the desire to impress a "dear little girl" led him to forge bank notes and checks.

Many of these bogus notes and checks turned up in several surrounding counties, a fact that would haunt Shotwell for many years.

Within a week of beginning his "crime spree," he was jailed in the Mount Pleasant jail but was quickly bailed out by his father. Authorities from Collin and Ellis Counties, however, had their own warrants issued for his arrest, and he found himself back in jail and his father unable to obtain additional bail.

Most rural Texas county jails operated on a two-term court calendar during the late 1800s, and Shotwell remained in jail for six months until the next court date could be set. He was convicted of the charges and sentenced to six years "hard labor" in the Texas prison system.

A Victim of Revenge or Fourteen Years in Hell recalls the despair he felt in the darkened county jail cell after sentencing: the realization that at age seventeen he was facing a six-year sentence in prison with the possibility that authorities in at least two more counties would press additional charges against him in the future.

Within days he was transferred to Rusk prison and processed as Inmate #3479. His initial impression of Rusk was understandably negative, but he would later look back upon his time there with far more favor once he had served time on leased work crews.

At Rusk he was assigned his very first day to pull wagons across the inside yard and load them with lumber. That night he was assigned a cell with an old man serving a sixty-year sentence, virtually a life commitment to prison, and recalls the despair and hopelessness he saw in the old man.

His imprisonment at Rusk was temporary, however, and he was soon transferred to a convict lease wood camp near Alto, Texas, and assigned the duty of chopping one and one-half cords of wood per day for six days a week. Failure to produce the required amount of chopped wood would result in thirty-nine lashes with the strap.

The daily assignment of one and one-half cords of wood appears to have been a particularly severe requirement—later state reports would suggest that one cord per day was the average on the other camps.

Because of his extended time in county jail awaiting trial, he was in poor physical condition when he arrived at Alto, and his hands were immediately so bloody that they stuck to the handle of the axe at the end of the day.

He had been issued brogan shoes that didn't fit, and since the state didn't issue socks at Alto, his feet soon became swollen and scraped raw and he could barely stand or walk.

Like most lease camps, Alto was considered a temporary work assignment and living quarters were extremely primitive. The inmate housing at Alto consisted of a building one hundred feet long and twenty-four feet wide with a guard picket at one end so the inmates could be watched at night.

Meals consisted of spoiled bacon, boiled corn, and stale corn bread served on rusty tin plates. Shotwell claims that while assigned to the work camp he spent the first four years sleeping on the same straw bunk without changing mattresses and during that period was forced to live and work without a single bath. Clothing was never laundered and was replaced only when worn out. Socks were never issued, and inmates would often work extended periods, even in winter, barefoot when shoes were not available.

The guards, he alleged, were among the most brutal in the prison system. Convicts, being nearly worked to death, would often make the threat, usually uttered under breath to other inmates, that if they could live to get out of the camp, they would one day return to kill their tormentors.

Rarely did an ex-convict follow through on these threats, but according to Shotwell, the situation at Alto was so bad that one such incident did occur.

One young boy, of poor physique and unable to meet his daily work quotas, was serving a two-year term. During the first year, Shotwell estimated that the boy was held down at least twenty-five times and administered the maximum thirty-nine lashes with the result that the inmate nearly went crazy. In his torment, the youngster threatened to live another year to discharge and then return and kill the whipping captain.

He did, in fact, survive his sentence and regained his health after discharge and obtained a pistol. Knowing that the captain responsible for his beatings rode the steam train to Wells twice a month to pick up the guards' payroll, he plotted his revenge. Only he picked a date one day too late.

The day after the captain actually made the round trip by train, this former inmate from Alto piled rail ties across the tracks in a manner that would force the train to stop. The passengers disembarked to remove the ties, and the ex-convict shot and killed a dentist thinking he was the captain.

He was caught, sentenced to death, and hung for murder. According to Shotwell, the youngster stood on the gallows and as a result of his brutal experiences at the Alto wood camp, was reported to have said: "I killed the wrong man and I'm sorry for it. I was driven to murder. Tell those officers at the wood camp that I'll meet them, every one, in hell."

After six years at the Alto wood camp, Shotwell was himself released from prison. Immediately upon release, however, authorities from Collin County appeared and ordered him rearrested for a forged twenty-five-dollar check he had cashed in that county.

He was sentenced to another six years "hard labor."

He returned to Rusk a second time as an understandably very bitter young man, facing another sentence similar to his first. Upon his arrival he was initially assigned to the foundry inside the Rusk walls as a molder and paired with an infamous train robber and murderer from Fort Worth named George Moore.

This time the living and working conditions at Rusk penitentiary seemed far better when compared to his previous work camp experiences. Comparing conditions inside the main unit at Rusk to his experiences in the Alto work camp, he would write: "I must honestly admit that I have no complaint as to the treatment of convicts inside the Rusk prison. Convicts at that place receive plenty of good, wholesome food, the sanitary conditions are of the very best, and the convicts are not overworked."

Like his first sentence, however, his initial stay at Rusk was short and temporary. Within a few months he was reassigned to another leased work camp near Cameron, Texas, picking cotton in the summer and chopping wood during the winter months.

His time in "hell" was only continuing. If he had thought his years at the Alto wood camp were horrendous, the conditions at Cameron were even more so.

At Cameron, he alleges, typical meals consisted of spoiled hog head, stale corn bread, and coffee brewed from burned corn bread crust.

Even more revolting is his assertion that work conditions were so brutal at Cameron that inmates routinely chopped off fingers, hands, toes, and even feet to escape the work crews. The self-mutilations became so rampant that Shotwell claims the guards started refusing to remove the maimed inmates from the work squads. When that happened, Shotwell claims, some desperate inmates even resorted to putting out their eyes so they could not be forced into the cotton rows.

Self-mutilations in the prison field crews were reported until well into the 1940s, however the rare and extreme act of self-blinding was almost unheard of.

The Texas prison system during those years attempted to "police and monitor" the private industries that were leasing state prisoners, but the efforts were almost universally denounced by the men who were subjected to the lease conditions.

One of those efforts, an intentionally high-profile attempt, was the use of state prison inspectors who would periodically visit the work camps, "talk" with the prisoners, and then report their findings to the state prison board.

Without exception, the convict narratives of the lease period claim these inspectors were simply sent out to the lease camps to produce a report indicating favorable living and work conditions for the prisoners being leased out by the state.

Shotwell also denounces these inspectors in *A Victim of Revenge or Fourteen Years in Hell*. He condemns these officials as nothing more than common criminals who were "on the take."

At the Cameron lease camp, Shotwell claims, "when the inspector made his monthly appearance, we would rather have seen the devil." On one occasion, looking at the emaciated, sickly, and obviously overworked convicts lined up in front of him, the inspector sarcastically observed:

> How are you thieves getting treated? I can see that you are well fed. You are getting fatter than I am. Then he would say: "Captain, be sure and give them plenty of work. If any of them begin to shirk, don't spare the leather, for I find, in the convict business, that the using of the leather is just as essential as feeding." On one occasion there was one of the men who told the inspector about the conditions under which we were compelled to exist. The inspector sneered and as he looked him over, said: "Now look here, what do you think you thieves deserve—the Menger hotel in San Antonio? You stuck-up cuss, I'll teach you something. Here, captain, take this man out and give him 39 lashes and maybe next time I come here he will remember me."

That inmate, according to Shotwell, was later given one of the most brutal beatings he ever witnessed in prison, and the following day the already sick convict was forced to work his regular schedule with blood soaking through his shirt and covered with flies.

The fact that the Texas prison system did attempt to monitor the conditions at the convict lease camps, even if they were cover-up attempts, during the period of Shotwell's incarceration from 1895 through 1909 does suggest that the prison system was at least sensitive to the charges of abuse and corruption in the camps.

Prior to 1910 many of the annual reports issued by the prison board to the Texas legislature are filled with these "favorable" accounts of the conditions of Texas inmates under the supervision of private leasers.

But not all prison board members were completely oblivious to the realities of convict work camps in Texas at the turn of the century. Interspersed through those annual reports are signals that the lease system and the inspectors who monitored the work camps were not reporting a completely accurate picture of the camp conditions.

Shotwell's allegations in *A Victim of Revenge or Fourteen Years in Hell* were published as a condemnation of what he saw as a brutal and corrupt state policy of extending slavery by sentencing Texas prisoners to "hard labor" in lease work camps. Specifically, he focused on the period of his own incarceration in those camps—an imprisonment that ended finally in 1909.

Ironically, it was the official state report issued one year after his release that would lead to the abolishment of the system he so thoroughly detested and hated.

In 1910 a massive state document titled *Report of the Penitentiary Investigating Committee including All Exhibits and Testimony Taken by the Committee* was published by the Texas House of Representatives. Shotwell does not indicate if he was aware of or familiar with the condemning document, but it verified the very abuses and corruption he so angrily alleged in *A Victim of Revenge or Fourteen Years in Hell.*

That report is credited with the abolishment of the convict lease system in Texas. Some of the excerpts included:

> Collaborated testimony of convicts show instances of brutal treatment by guards, the convicts fearing to report such treatment to superior officers lest the guards wreak vengeance upon them when further opportunity is afforded by the isolation of the fields.[1]

> The treatment of the men on the farms is wholly in the hands of the sergeant in charge, who if he possessed a drop of the milk of human kindness in his heart, can do much for the comfort of those dependent upon him for care and protection. If he be other than a man of kind but firm disposition and incapable of grasping the great responsibility of his position, he can make life not only most unpleasant, but almost unbearable for that unfortunate class of our population serving a sentence in the State penitentiary.[2]

> We recommend that the contract and labor share farm system be abolished not later than January 1, 1912, and that all convicts be kept and worked in the prisons and upon the State farms....[3]

But while assigned to the work camp at Cameron, John Shotwell did not resort to self-mutilation like many of the desperate men he worked with. He did, however, attempt unsuccessfully to escape on several occasions, actions resulting in his being classified a high-risk inmate.

Then, he claims, the true hell really began. He was transferred to the infamous Calvert Coal Mines.

In a statewide system of convict lease camps with horrendous reputations, the worst assignment a Texas prisoner could get was a transfer to the Calvert Coal Mines. Considered by most inmates to be a "death camp," the Calvert lease camp probably most represented the philosophy that convicted felons were expendable sources of labor to be worked until they were physically broken or dead.

At Calvert, guards would tell the inmates the draft animals they worked with were worth more because they cost money to replace while there was an endless source of convicts available for lease to the mining company.

Finally, at the end of the line, John Shotwell found himself transferred to those very coal mines near Calvert where he mined ore for the Houston & Texas Central Railroad Company. "Of all the horrors that I had ever witnessed," he later recalled, "there was none to compare with those coal mines."

Surprisingly, Shotwell reported that the food at this camp was good, even exceptional, but only because the railroad and the prison guards wanted healthy convicts that they could work to death in the mines. Later reports, including the 1910 annual prison report, would document that most of the food made available to inmates at Calvert was unfit for human consumption.

Inmate deaths did occur almost daily inside the mines as the result of unsafe and dangerous working conditions. One summer Shotwell and other inmates were building a levee on the Brazos River to prevent mine flooding. The sun was so hot and the inmates so overworked, he claimed, that prisoners were passing out from heat exhaustion and sunstroke. The typical reaction of the guards, he alleges, was to strip the inmates and flog them with a strap to verify they were really unconscious and not faking to avoid work.

It was during this work assignment that he jumped into the Brazos River one day and escaped amid a hail of bullets to the other side. There, free of the dogs and guards, he traveled cross-country until he found a house and stole some food and a rifle.

After hiding twenty days in the brush, he stole clothes from another home and then left Texas on an extended journey that included stops at Denver, Omaha, Chicago, and Kansas City. It was in Chicago that he attempted to mislead Texas prison officials by writing them a letter informing them he was living in Denver.

As a result of his letter, the Texas prison commission issued a national alert for his arrest and sent wanted posters displaying his photograph to every train station in the country.

Shotwell, who had traveled from Chicago to Kansas City, was recognized and jailed. A guard from the Rusk penitentiary was dispatched to escort him back to Texas in chains. Just inside the Texas state line, he claims, that guard fell asleep and a sympathetic train conductor allowed him to escape.

The horrendous reputation of the state prison system was so well known throughout Texas, Shotwell contends, that many citizens were privately sympathetic to the plight of escaped convicts.

Escaping from the train still handcuffed, Shotwell stumbled all night in the darkness until he found an elderly couple living in an isolated farmhouse. Explaining to them that the leg irons were the result of a "show he was in" and that the keys had been "lost," he managed to convince them to file the cuffs from his legs.

He spent two days with the kindly couple and despite his taking advantage of their hospitality and concern, later wrote that their kindness gave him a new appreciation of the human race after his time in the work camps and coal mine.

This time he "tramped" his way on the railroads through San Antonio south to Mexico where he worked selling stocks for a silver mine in San Luis Potosi. He fell in love with a "Spanish Queen" who later betrayed his identity to Mexican officials, resulting in his arrest. This same jaded lover, however, helped him escape jail once again, and this time he escaped in a rail car traveling north to Jefferson, Texas.

His luck wasn't any better there, and he was betrayed again. At Jefferson he met an ex-convict he had known at Rusk and was turned in for a ten-dollar reward.

Another prison representative was dispatched from Rusk, and this time the guard made sure Shotwell completed the trip back to prison, and he served the remainder of his second sentence locked away with no privileges and no communication with the outside world. Just before that sentence ended, he was transferred back to Ellis County and given an additional two-year sentence for checks forged there. On the way back to Rusk, Shotwell tried to kill himself by jumping off the train.

This time he was assigned to another convict lease camp in Hill County working the cotton fields. He remained there until his health began failing and he was transferred back to the main prison unit at Rusk. He finished his third sentence, he claims, a man broken down by years of excessive work, abuses, and maltreatment.

He was released the final time at age thirty-six after serving three sentences totaling fourteen years in Texas prisons. Texas, he claimed, had taken its "tithe" from him.

A Victim of Revenge or Fourteen Years in Hell is a personal account filled with bitterness and anger, yet John Shotwell did succeed in portraying the hellish conditions of Texas lease camps in graphic and convincing terms.

Shotwell's early teenage years prior to his incarceration must have included a good education, at least for the late 1800s. *A Victim of Revenge or Fourteen Years in Hell* is a well-written narrative in which Shotwell vents the bitterness of his prison years but manages to temper his anger and

John Shotwell spent fourteen years in Texas prison work camps during the convict lease period. After his release, he published his memoir and included this undated photo of himself with his daughter.
Shotwell, John, *A Victim of Revenge or Fourteen Years in Hell* (San Antonio: E.J. Jackson Co., 1909)

frustration with often very objective descriptions of the conditions inmates were subjected to in the lease work camps.

John Shotwell failed in his desire to rally public outrage at the practices inside the state prison system—it would be over a half-century before that would occur. In addition to his desire to expose the brutality and corruption he witnessed doing three sentences in Texas work camps, he claims his memoir is an effort to dissuade young men from following his footsteps.

Near the end of his narrative, he reiterates his desire to "inform the public of the excesses of the prison system" and to "dissuade would-be criminals from following their impulses."

> The little sparks of illustrations and kind advice that I have scattered throughout this little book I hope some day will be fanned into burning flames of nobility in the souls of many young people. My future life, if nothing happens to prevent me, will be spent in the sincere interest of fallen humanity. If I am successful in

my undertakings of upraising and restoring to their proper places in life, fallen humanity, then, and never until then, will I reach the summit of my humane ambition.

While he failed in exposing to the public the brutalities of the convict lease system, many of the allegations he made in *A Victim of Revenge or Fourteen Years in Hell* were later substantiated in the 1910 legislative report, which did lead to the abolishment of that very system he so detested.

His success in preventing young men from becoming criminals is more difficult to judge. His impassioned narrative of his own prison experiences during the Texas convict lease period, however, almost certainly must have touched in some way every reader who picked up *A Victim of Revenge or Fourteen Years in Hell.*

---

1   *Report of the Penitentiary Investigating Committee including All Exhibits and Testimony Taken by the Committee, Published by Order of the House of Representatives, August 1910*, pg. 12.
2   Ibid., pg. 14.
3   Ibid., pg. 16.

Chapter Two

Where Hogs Feasted on the Corpses of Convicts

Various sources refer to the trail of unmarked graves along the Texas State Railroad and other work camps where Texas prisoners toiled during the convict lease system. Few accounts, however, go into the gruesome details as does the narrative of John Shotwell, who served fourteen years in prison and on various work camps from 1895 to 1909.

For six years Shotwell worked outside of Rusk at a wood camp near Alto, Texas. There, he and the other convicts were assigned the job of cutting cords of wood to be burned down into charcoal for the ore smelters at the penitentiary in Rusk.

Of the numerous convict wood camps that sprang up and moved around as needed, the one near Alto seems to have been particularly brutal. It was here that Shotwell recorded inmates were required to cut one and one-half cords of wood a day—a half-cord more than at the other camps. Alto was, according to Shotwell, a camp where inmates were literally worked and beaten to death regularly.

At the time he was assigned to the work camp, Alto itself was a small and isolated community in East Texas located on the highest point between the Neches and the Angelina Rivers.

The camp, however, was located outside Alto, and Shotwell describes one of the low-lying areas in which the prisoners worked and its grisly history:

> Far out in the swamps of the eastern part of Cherokee county, within a clearing surrounded on all sides by forests of dense pine, in the center of which rises the lone figure of an immense pine tree, is situated what is known as the "Lone Pine Graveyard," a burial ground of convicts, where many of my companions at the wood camp nearby were laid in shallow graves during the six years I spent at the place. [1]

Shotwell creates an image of that single pine tree serving as both marker and memorial to the convict dead buried around it. "Desolate to the very extreme of desolation, the gaunt figure of the sentinel pine stands majestic in its vigil over Texas convict dead."

In an era where the prevailing philosophy was "mules cost money, men don't," Shotwell reports little respect was given the state wards who were buried at Lone Pine Graveyard.

> No words of love or reverence were spoken at those graves—no funeral hymns were sung. No relatives or mourning friends followed the dead march to the grave. No markers but the pine stumps on which were wrought the labor of the prison gang, designate the spot where each of God's unfortunates that died a martyr to Texas magnificence is drifting into mould. No visitants shed tears or deck with flowers the graves within that desolate spot, the largest convict camp burial ground in Texas. The wind that sighs through the branches of the lonesome pine, or the quavering cry of the wolf is the only sound that breaks the stillness of the "Graveyard of the Lone Pine."

Shotwell also creates a dismal image of the final moments leading to the burial of the bodies. No elaborate horse-drawn hearse existed here; the deceased inmates were carried out to the clearing in a mule-drawn water cart. Not bothering to build even crude pine coffins, the prison system simply used old wooden boxes previously discarded.

> Their casket was a goods box; if it were too large well and good; if it were too small the corpse was made to fit the coffin. Often I have seen a guard put his foot upon a corpse and crush it into the narrow confines that the lid might be nailed down.

So random were the burials that no records were kept with regards to location or even names.

> Bodies were buried, some with head to the east and feet to the west; some facing north or south. Graves were soon lost track of, and sometimes when digging a new one, an old skeleton would be unearthed. So shallow were the graves that sometimes hogs would root the bodies up.

One inmate who escaped anonymity in his burial at the Lone Pine Graveyard was the young convict described in *A Victim of Revenge or Fourteen Years in Hell* as the abused youth who survived his prison sentence and discharged only to return with a gun and kill the wrong man on a train from Rusk. That young ex-convict, according to Shotwell, died on the gallows boasting he would see the guards from the Alto wood camp in hell.

Those who were buried at the Lone Pine Graveyard had died, according to Shotwell, from other than natural causes. "Many committed suicide. Still more were killed in attempting escape, and a few were victims to outbreaks of pestilence."

Today Alto is far less isolated than it was a century ago when John Shotwell was assigned to the wood camp there. Located on a major highway between Lufkin and Rusk, Alto is a community connected to the cattle ranching and the oil and gas industries.

In East Texas, however, lumber has always been a primary industry, and today the loaded lumber trucks continue to drive through the town on their way to the sawmills. But the lumber industry, like everything else, has changed since Shotwell's time here.

The Lone Pine Graveyard, where hogs feasted on the corpses of convicts, is probably lost forever. As he wrote in *A Victim of Revenge or Fourteen Years in Hell*, "No boundaries were ever kept. The camp has been moved to other timber and the cemetery forgotten. Nothing now remains to mark it as a burial ground but the figure of the guardian pine."

And today, even the pine "tombstone" is gone.

---

1   Shotwell, John, *A Victim of Revenge or Fourteen Years in Hell*, pg. 12.

Chapter Three

Who Was John Henry and Why Do Inmates Call Him Johnnie?

Institutional food has always been the target of criticism and complaints. The military has known that fact for years, and school cafeterias are the butt of food jokes at all grade levels. Inmates in state prison units are no less vocal about the quality of their food—probably more critical than most.

The perceived poor quality of their food has led to rumors, stories, allegations, and even some slang terms. One of those is the term "Johnnie." Outside trustys, such as tractor drivers, often leave for the fields each morning with their "Johnnies" in hand.

A "Johnnie" is a sack lunch, usually packed with a couple of sandwiches, fruit, and whatever else the food steward chooses to include. During periods of unrest, riots, or "shakedowns," when the inmates are locked in their cells for extended periods, a cart is rolled down the tiers and "Johnnies" are handed in through the bars to the inmates inside the cells.

But while inmates, guards, and civilian personnel inside the Texas prisons today use the term freely, few if any probably know what it means or where the expression came from.

The narratives of the convict lease years—spanning from 1875 to 1925—give us an idea of how important food was to these men. Given the brutal daily work quotas of seven tons of coal, three hundred pounds of cotton, or one and one-half cords of wood, these convicts needed decent food and plenty of it.

But they never got it.

The 1910 legislative report details the woefully inadequate food supply and food preparation facilities at the work camps. As to menu, the common observation was that the men received some type of pork meat (very often described as "spoiled"), boiled corn, and stale corn bread (also often described as "spoiled").

Even today the Texas prison fare is predominantly pork with some poultry. Hog fat is used today to cook virtually anything placed in a pan or on a grill. It is even used to "flavor" vegetables stewing on the serving line. But as bad as prison food may be perceived today, it is vastly improved both in quality and selection as compared to the convict lease years.

In the 1800s pork was almost always mentioned when convicts recalled their food in the camps. Various descriptions emerged: boiled hog's head; bacon "cakes" almost completely fat; raw, spoiled bacon slabs.

Even on the prison farms that harvested produce crops, the inmates reported they seldom received vegetables other than corn. Even the bread relied upon corn—often from the same dried staple as was used to feed the livestock. On occasion, the narratives suggest, the harvest of crops would temporarily supplement the meals with beans, peas, potatoes, and other vegetables. But that was rare.

Midday and evening meals were usually the same fare with the nightly meals simply warmed leftovers from the lunch menu. Breakfast usually consisted of some type of bacon and corn bread or rolls with sorghum or molasses and occasionally coffee in the mornings.

But the convicts who worked in the fields, mines, and lumber camps often walked or ran considerable distances from the camp to where they spent the day working. Rather than consume time making a round trip back to the camp for the midday meal, prison officials would send the meals out to the convicts.

Bill Mills, who served a quarter century in various Texas prisons, gives us a clue as to the origin of the term "Johnnie." That expression, he claims, was originally "John Henry," and dates back at least to the Civil War.

According to Mills, "Our dinner was brought to us over there. It is known as John Henry on the turn row (an area where plows or other equipment turn around). The prison wagon that brought the meals was called John Henry. The reason for this, I was told by an old guard who began guarding prisoners in 1868 was: the first dinner wagon was driven by an old man called John Henry, and since then the name John Henry is very precious to the hungry prisoners."[1]

Likewise, Beecher Deason recalled in the 1920s, "It was nearing noon when I heard a convict next to me yell 'John Henry' on the turn row. I looked up and saw a trusty coming in a wagon. He had our dinner…It was in cans ranging in size from five to twenty gallons, and consisted of beans or peas, bacon, corn bread and sorghum molasses."[2]

In the late 1890s J.S. Calvin reported another food term that has all but disappeared from contemporary inmate slang. Calvin reported that his John Henry often included a "duffer." A "duffer" was a biscuit that started as a large glob of dough and was allowed to rise into a large mound of bread. Midday John Henrys often consisted of bacon, a "duffer," and little else.

Duffers were also used at the morning meal, and Calvin recalls, "the duffer was about a half of an ordinary loaf of light bread and if your appetite called for more bread you got corn bread to finish out your breakfast on."[3]

As late as the 1970s, very, very old lifers who had served time in Texas prisons in the 1940s and 50s would occasionally still use the term "duffer." It is almost never heard today.

But not a day passes in Texas prisons that the term "Johnnie" isn't used somewhere on some unit by any number of inmates, guards, and staff. And whether they realize it or not, they are using a prison slang expression that dates back to probably before 1868 when old John Henry hitched his mules and hauled food out to the convicts slaving in the fields of Texas prisons.

---

1   Mills, Bill, *25 Years Behind Prison Bars*, pg. 15.
2   Deason, Beecher, *Seven Years in Texas Prisons*, pp. 2-3.
3   Calvin, J.S., *Buried alive, or, A term in the Texas State Prison, 1898-1902: a chapter from real life*, pg. 30.

Chapter Four

(1885-1891)

The Texas Convict

The Texas Prison Memoir of Andrew L. George

*Oh the many long nights and days that dragged out over
me. Many were the times that I wished I was dead and
had made up my mind to commit suicide but after more
than five years had passed the Captain sent for me and
when I went to his office he told me that I was pardoned.
I will leave it to the reader to explain the feeling. I was
turned loose with five dollars to face this cold old world.*

In 1885 Andrew George arrived at Huntsville with a commuted sentence of life imprisonment. Some would have considered him lucky; his original sentence had been death by hanging, and twice that summer George had come within hours of swinging from the hangman's noose in Lavaca County.

George arrived at Huntsville, like many prisoners, adamantly proclaiming his innocence of the charges against him while also wondering if he could spend the rest of his natural life in prison without committing suicide.

At the depths of his despair, when he was actively pondering taking his own life, he received an unexpected pardon from the governor based upon another man's dying confession that substantiated George's claims of innocence.

Andrew George spent five and one-half years doing a life sentence inside the walls of the Huntsville prison unit, and in 1895 he published his reminiscences in a small booklet titled *The Texas Convict: Sketches of the Penitentiary, Convict Farms and Railroads, Together with Poems.*

The title is somewhat misleading; George served his entire sentence inside the walls at Huntsville and never actually worked on a convict farm or railroad. But his narrative, *The Texas Convict*, provides a rare and well-written description of inmate life inside the central state penitentiary in the 1880s.

Given the fact that Andrew George's protestations of innocence were later substantiated with an unconditional pardon and he had been imprisoned nearly six years for a crime he didn't commit, *The Texas Convict* presents an objective look at the Texas prison system from 1895 to 1891 in a manner surprisingly free of anger and bitterness, although in very emotional terms.

His narrative spends only a brief two pages proclaiming his innocence and false imprisonment before providing a description of his prison life and the general conditions inside the unit at Huntsville.

The tragic circumstances of his false conviction and his prison sentence were only two episodes of a life that had already been marked with tragedy from his earliest days.

He was born near Moulton, Texas, midway between Houston and San Antonio, on December 12, 1862. His father died when Andrew was three years old, and at age eight he and his three siblings were orphaned with the death of their mother. The children were separated into different homes, and Andrew moved to DeWitt County and attended school in Yorktown.

He does not indicate how much schooling he received, but the quality of his writing in *The Texas Convict* suggests he was relatively well educated for that period.

At the age of eighteen he moved west and worked as a cowboy for three years—a period in which he later recalled he had become involved with men of "questionable character" and had begun to develop bad personal habits. While in his early twenties, he became tired of the "wild life" and returned to Lavaca County in the fall of 1884.

That "wild life," his bad personal habits, and the men of questionable character he had associated with followed him to Lavaca County. George was in the company of two shady associates in 1884 when a barroom they were visiting erupted into a brawl during which a local citizen was shot and killed.

Despite his claims of innocence, George was arrested, tried, and convicted for the murder. The Lavaca County jury sentenced him to "hang by the neck until dead," and on two occasions during the spring and summer of 1885 he came within hours of his executioin being carried out. He was sentenced on April 13 of that year to be hanged on June 26. Three days before his scheduled execution, Governor Ireland ordered a stay and rescheduled his hanging for August 6. Then, on August 2, the governor commuted his sentence from death to life imprisonment.

On August 20, 1885, he was chained by the neck to another prisoner and transferred to the Texas state penitentiary at Huntsville to begin, in his words, "a life worse than death itself."

In many ways the prison at Huntsville has changed very little since its inception in 1849. The massive brick walls sit where they were originally built, only interior modifications and other functional and cosmetic changes have taken place. One exception is the removal of the original massive clock tower over the entrance gate.

But Andrew George, in *The Texas Convict*, creates an image of the foreboding walls and entrance gate as seen by a new convict arriving at nighttime when only the flames of lanterns provided an indication of what lay inside those dreaded walls:

> Assisted by a convict trusty, who met us here with a lantern, we were marched probably half a mile to the outside gate of a high wall which surrounds all the buildings of the penitentiary. This wall, built of stone, is known as the outer one, and is four feet thick and twenty feet high. In addition to this there is an inner one of the same dimensions. The entrance through these walls is closed by two large iron doors which are never at the same time opened and are locked and unlocked by a convict trusty. Just outside the first gate, a few steps from it, is a small round building, a sentry box, in which there is always a guard, gun in hand or within easy reach.
>
> ...and we pass through, never to return, so says our sentence, and to our minds at that time nothing seemed to reasonably justify us in believing that it would be altered.

He includes in *The Texas Convict* descriptions of the town of Huntsville as it appeared in 1885 and describes the harsh and inhumane conditions of convicts leased out to one of the farms "bordering the Brazos River." He does not name the camp but describes it as a 4,000-acre farm where corn, cotton, cane, oats, and potatoes were raised:

> ...all the work is done by convicts presided over sometimes by very cruel tyrants in the person of the guards, and are compelled to work very hard, are poorly clothed and fed and subjected to the dangerous malaria that abounds in this section of the state, especially on the river bottoms, and many succumb to its deadly poisonous effects, while others, to make them

complete tasks which are more than their skill and endurance can accomplish, are whipped so unmercifully by cruel guards that they are injured for life or perhaps die from this horrible punishment. A railroad passes through this farm, from which they are subjected to the mortification of being gazed at daily by their more fortunate fellows, as miserable and servilely [*sic*] they toil through the long hot summer or cold winter days, a guard with gun in hand near by, ready to shoot them should they make an effort to escape.

To emphasize the terrible conditions of this work camp, George concludes: "Surely it is no sacrilege to say that a convict gets a foretaste of that awful place spoken of in the Bible as Hell."

Probably based upon the accounts of other inmates returning from the fields, he also describes a wood camp. He identifies it only as "located in the piney wood region of the state," which means it could have been one of any number of sawmill camps leased from the state and operated by inmate laborers.

His narrative of the sawmill camp is unique in that it includes one of the few descriptions of the ball and chain as a punishment device, and he also describes the infamous "spur" that inmates who were considered high risks for escape attempts were required to wear in the fields. After an inmate had tried to escape, the guards would "spur" him by placing a metal band around one or both ankles.

"That spur," according to George, "consisted of a shank attached to an iron band riveted around the ankle and so shaped, that it turns up in the manner of a rooster's spur, and is about six inches long, two of these thus fastened to the iron band, one in front and one behind, that effectually prevents a convict making any speed at running away, as it is with much difficulty and annoyance he is enabled to move about sufficiently quick enough to complete his task."

His own late-night arrival at Huntsville, however, brought about the removal of the hated neck chains that had been riveted onto him at the Lavaca County jail. During the two-day train trip, the chains had remained around his neck, even in Houston where he had spent the previous night.

The first morning inside the prison walls at Huntsville, his head and face were completely shaven and he was served a breakfast of sour corn bread and boiled bacon with coffee. Despite being famished, he recalls, the food was so bad he could not eat it.

Then, in one of the most emotional passages of *The Texas Convict*, Andrew George describes that moment when he first truly realized he was a convict in the state prison system serving a life sentence.

After being stripped and issued striped convict clothing, he writes, he had that moment of crushing humiliation so degrading that he wished he had kept one of the earlier appointments he had had with the hangman's noose. The cheap prison shirt and pants had his name stenciled across the back in large black letters with a red dot the size of a silver dollar below his name. The red dot announced to the prison world, guards and other inmates alike, that he was serving a life sentence and should be watched closely.

His humiliation was a common theme throughout *The Texas Convict*—enhanced possibly by the fact he knew he was innocent of the crime for which he had been sentenced to prison.

In what must have been a gut wrenching self-examination, he recalled: "...when I was alone I looked at my stripes and then at the iron bars and asked myself 'is this A.L. George,' if so, how came him in such a place as this, and how long has he got to stay here...."

Then, in a short passage, he describes the despair and heartbreak at recalling the memory of his mother, who had passed away when he was only eight years old:

> ...is this the kind of man his mother died praying for him to make. I say no; no! bad company has put me in this place. I felt like lifting my eyes heavenward and crying "O mother, at home in heaven, with earnest prayer, I ask that your eyes may not look earthward on the failure of your task."

After issuance of his prison clothing, he was taken to the third floor of the factory, issued a job in the shoe shop, and given a work quota of completing five pairs of brogan shoes a day. On his way to the third floor that first day, he recalled he saw for the first time the legendary gunslinger John Wesley Hardin at work in the tailor shop.

George apparently adjusted well to prison life at Huntsville, at least with regards to surviving the daily routines. He worked in the shoe shop for two years before being promoted to the machine department. There he quickly mastered his job and began earning extra privileges such as using the visiting yard on Sundays.

But while he was making institutional adjustments well, the humiliation, disgrace, and despair he had felt that second evening in his cell never left him. He recalls, "there were many times that I wished I was dead."

After serving five and one-half years of a life sentence at Huntsville for a crime he didn't commit, Andrew George decided to commit suicide.

Then, at that moment of deepest despair, he was summoned to the captain's office and informed the governor had issued him an unconditional pardon.

One of the men of "questionable character" he had accompanied to the Lavaca County barroom the night of the murder had recently died. On his deathbed he had issued a sworn statement that he had been the killer and that Andrew George had been innocent of the charges and falsely convicted.

While a dying man's deathbed confession under those circumstances is often considered suspect, this admission of guilt resulted in Andrew George being absolved of all charges against him.

Based upon that witnessed deathbed statement, Governor Ross had issued a full pardon to Andrew L. George on January 22, 1890. The wording of the pardon left no doubt as to the basis of the executive action. The document stated that the pardon "...completely exonerates the said George of all complicity or blame, and the sentiment is universal of those, cognizant of the fact that he is guiltless."

After serving five and one-half years of an apparently erroneous conviction, Andrew George was released from prison and given a cheap suit of clothes and five dollars.

With that, he used his experiences to become a respected prison reform advocate and to write passionately about the dangers of leading a criminal lifestyle. Among the issues he campaigned for were vocational training inside the prison walls and employment opportunities being made available to ex-convicts upon release. A century before federally mandated court injunctions forced the expansion of the state prison system to more than 125 prison units in Texas, Andrew George warned of the need to address the crime problem or "Texas would be compelled to have six prisons instead of two." Obviously nobody listened.

Without rehabilitation efforts inside the prison, he maintained, the penitentiary at Huntsville was "only a mill for turning out criminals to prey on our community."

The Texas Convict is a short, well-written account of his time in Texas prison—surprisingly portrayed without vindictiveness or resentment. And although *The Texas Convict* provides a valuable description of Texas prison life in the 1880s, it is Andrew George's eloquent portrayal of the dehumanizing humiliation he suffered while being incarcerated that makes his narrative so powerful.

After his release in 1891 Andrew George toured several states lecturing on prison reform, hardly a popular issue or high priority in Texas during the final years of the nineteenth century. Little else is known of him or his later life.

Chapter Five

Thirty-Nine Lashes with the "Bat"

No aspect of serving time during the convict lease period or the early years of the state farms was more hated or feared than the use of the "bat." Virtually every convict account from that period describes, in grisly detail, the implement and its use.

John Wesley Hardin gave one of the earliest accounts of its use after his second escape attempt. Hardin reports that in 1879 guards removed him from his cell, stripped him, tied short ropes to his arms and feet, and then used them to spread him face down on the floor and hold him. He then received thirty-nine lashes resulting in his back "quivering and bleeding."

It appears each disciplinary captain designed and had constructed his own version of the "bat," but the various descriptions list it as being a leather strap eighteen inches to three feet long and three to five inches wide and attached to a wooden handle one to three feet long (hence the name "bat") for a total length of up to five feet. Descriptions of the leather list it as tough, "sole" leather up to three-ply thickness.

Just the mention of the "bat" would usually change the behavior of the toughest convicts of the period. Even in the hands of an experienced captain, it seldom failed to draw blood, and the discoloration of the leather led to the instrument being called various names: Red Bet, Old Caesar, Black Dan, Red Heifer, and Louisiana Fan.

While the physical damage from use of the bat cannot be overstated, the fact is that prison officials also used, very effectively, the psychological effects of the instrument to discipline inmates.

Officials would usually wait until end of the work day to call the inmate being punished out for the whipping. The other inmates would also be called out and usually ordered to form a ring so they could watch the whipping. The man being punished would be placed in the center of the ring, and many accounts from this period describe even the hardened convicts falling to their knees, begging and pleading to avoid the lashes.

The man would then be ordered to lower his pants and lie down face first on the ground or floor with the warning that refusal to do so would result in even more blows. Usually the men would do so, but sometimes they would be shaking so badly they couldn't comply. There was often a loss of body control and the men would soil themselves before the strapping began.

Then, to further the psychological effects of the whipping on the other inmates, several would be selected to hold the victim down. Usually short ropes or chains would be attached to the convict's arms and feet, and the other inmates would pull him out "spread-eagled" while a fifth would be ordered to sit on his head to hold him down and smother his screams. Bill Mills recalled that as a new inmate he was ordered to do so, and the captain told him: "Old boy, you had better get his damned head down so he can't holler so loud." Mills was so afraid, he nearly smothered the man by forcing his face in the sand.[1]

In an attempt to turn the inmates against each other, the captain would usually order the convict's close friends to hold him down. Under the threat of being whipped themselves for noncompliance, they would almost always do so. Often the officers would use black inmates to hold down a white inmate being strapped in order to further humiliate or insult the man being whipped; or they would order white inmates to constrain a black inmate being punished.

In 1892 Charles Favor recalled watching his first strapping: "The convict lay down on the floor and all was silent: breathlessly I listened, and all at once there was a sudden, violent meeting of the strap and human flesh, and a scream, a wild scream for mercy, but another lick was the reply, and I counted twenty-five. The man was told, like a dog, to go to his bunk, and to it he went. There were many others whipped while I was under the gun. How my heart would go out in

Almost all inmate narratives during the convict lease period described the use of the "bat." Charles Favor offers this illustration but most written descriptions indicated other inmates always held the punished man down by the hands and feet. Favor, Charles A., *Twenty-Two Months in the Texas Penitentiary* (Corsicana, TX: Democrat Print, 1900).

sympathy to them as I would hear them beg in child-like simplicity for mercy!"[2]

Six years later J.S. Calvin would likewise recall his first witnessing of the use of the bat: "He made Smith pull off his pants and lie down on the floor, face downward, and then called four other big fellows and made them get on him and hold him down, while he hit him 30 licks on his naked hide with that murderous strap of leather. To hear the piteous yells and groans of that poor fellow as he writhed in agony...."[3]

When the strapping was finished, any other "troublesome" inmates would then be ordered to come forward and smell, or even lick, the sweat-stained, bloody leather strap as a warning.[4]

Usually the other inmates were forced to gather around and ordered to watch the beating, but sometimes the officials would strap an offender late at night so the other men would have to lie in their bunks and listen to the screams.

In the early 1900s J.L. Wilkinson recalled: "With ease I have heard the licks more than two hundred yards away; heard his victims beg and moan and yell like the spirits of the damned."[5]

While use of the bat was supposed to be regulated by prison policy, inmates claimed that on the isolated work camps and state farms, its administration was completely at the discretion of the punishing officer. In 1895 John Shotwell alleges the bat "was kept in a tub of water to give it extra weight."[6] Several narratives reported that sand would be sprinkled on the punished inmate's back or that the leather strap would be periodically drug through sand during administration to increase the pain.[7]

The officers who used the bat also became experts at finding the most effective and painful methods of applying the strap. Mills later wrote, "They would hit the prisoner one or two licks and then step across him to the other side and hit him in the same amount from that side. I thought it was very kind of the captain to change and not whip the man in the same place so much but soon learned that he did this in order that the other side might be getting sore so when he changed back again it would hurt worse," and that it typically took "eight to twelve minutes whipping a man."[8]

Charles Campbell, a decade earlier, recorded, "By bringing it over the head with a quick swing and giving it a jerk like popping a whip they can strip off the skin like peeling a cooked potato."[9]

Although some accounts like J.L. Wilkinson's *The Trans-Cedar lynching and the Texas Penitentiary* claim that seventy-five or even one hundred strokes could be applied in the 1800s, the most common limit of "licks" was reported as thirty-nine.

George Waverly Briggs, in his damning series of columns about the prison system in the *San Antonio Express*, made the use of the bat a public issue in 1909. As a result, the *1910 Report of the Penitentiary Investigating Committee* examined the policy of corporal punishment but recommended keeping the bat while trying to regulate its construction and application:

> ...whipping may be resorted to, but only on special order in writing from said board, or from such person or persons as it may designate in this respect....
>
> ...a leather strap, one end of which being encased in a wooden handle, shall be used, constructed thusly: The hand grip of the handle shall be six inches long, and the inner end of the handle shall encase one end of the strap four inches, securely; the strap beyond the handle shall be made of soft pliable leather, not more than three-sixteenths of an inch thick, two and one-half inches wide, and two feet long, and the end of

which shall be rounded and the edges well trimmed. The whipping shall be laid on no other part of the convict's body than the buttocks, and not more than fifteen licks shall be given to any convict on any one day.

No convict shall be whipped except in the presence of some citizen of the State, not directly employed by the penitentiary system…any violator guilty of a misdemeanor.…The camp physician shall examine the convict before being whipped, and shall witness the punishment.[10]

Shortly after the release of the 1910 report, the prison system does seem to have implemented some "official" changes in the administration of the bat including reducing the maximum number of lashes to twenty.

Bill Mills, in the period immediately after these changes were implemented, recalls that prison guards were aware of the new regulations but were just as effective at ignoring them as before: "He would change sides several times during the whipping, which was usually about twenty licks. That was all the state would allow. The doctor is required to watch the whipping and if any blood is seen he must stop the whipping …I have seen the doctor turn his back to the prisoner until about the eighteenth lash, then turn and see plenty of blood and then he would stop the captain at once. In this way he could say he stopped him when he saw blood."[11]

And on the farms and work camps, inmates continued to report that the new regulations were being ignored, with several claims that captains were whipping convicts with a trace chain inside a rubber hose.

By the early 1930s the prison system had been investigated once more, at the insistence of Governor Miriam Ferguson, and the use of the bat again challenged. In 1935 Lee

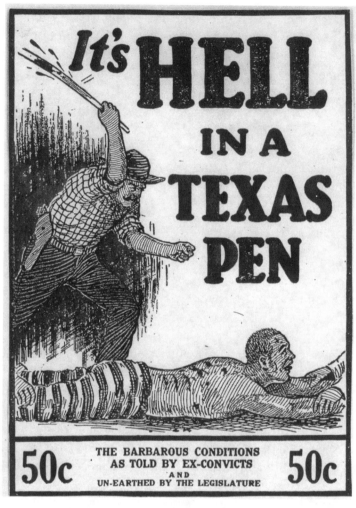

This pamphlet, published probably in the 1940s, was a collection of undocumented allegations against the prison system and a scrapbook of Texas newspaper articles concerning the brutality inside the prisons. The booklet does not list a party responsible for publishing it, a publisher, or even a date. The cover, however, is typical in portraying alleged brutality—almost always at the hands of an official using the "bat."

It's Hell in a Texas Pen, the barbarous conditions as told by ex-convicts and unearthed by the Legislature (Dallas?: 1925?), pamphlet on file at the Center for American History, University of Texas at Austin.

Simmons was appointed to head the prison system with orders to "clean it up."

Simmons, however, insisted on keeping the bat. "The average conception is that the use of the 'bat' in prison management is outmoded and belongs to the Dark Ages," he later wrote. "But, to my way of thinking, the alternative of solitary confinement as practiced in nearly all present-day prisons is inhuman and should not be tolerated. After every warning has failed, after every attempt at guidance has been rejected, corporal punishment should be used, but used for disciplinary purposes only."[12]

Comparing inmates to old horses, Simmons justified continuation of the use of the bat to the legislators: "Gentlemen, it's just like using spurs. You get on an old cow horse without spurs and you can't head even a milking-pen cow; but when you've got your spurs on, the old horse will do the job. And you don't have to use the spurs, because all he needs to know is that the spurs are there. It's the same with us and the bat."[13]

Simmons got his wish, and the legislature approved the continued use of the "Red Heifer" until into the 1940s. In 1957 Simmons would reflect, "But, after my resignation as general manager, the next legislature forbade the use of corporal punishment—in response to the urgings of misguided and ill-informed humanitarians."[14]

The infamous bat had finally been outlawed in Texas, as had the concept of corporal punishment. Subsequent allegations and investigations, however, would show that prison guards and officials found other ways to physically punish inmates until the 1980s.

But no matter how painful or brutal, probably no punishment ever devised came near the dreaded and hated effects of the "bat."

The hated and feared "bat." Usually 39 strokes would be applied to bare back and buttocks, but many inmate narratives report the limit of lashes was commonly ignored. The bat was used in Texas prisons until outlawed by the legislature in the 1940s. Photo by Gary Brown, courtesy of the Texas Prison Museum

1   Mills, Bill, *25 Years Behind Prison Bars*, pp. 13-14.
2   Favor, Charles A., *Twenty-Two Months in the Texas Penitentiary*, pp. 61-62.
3   Calvin, J.S., *Buried alive, or, A term in the Texas State Prison, 1898-1902: a chapter from real life*, pp. 49-50.
4   Ibid., pg. 14.
5   Wilkinson, J.L., *The Trans-Cedar lynching and the Texas Penitentiary*, pg. 80.
6   Shotwell, John, *A Victim of Revenge or Fourteen Years in Hell*, pg. 11.
7   *Report of the Penitentiary Investigating Committee including All Exhibits and Testimony Taken by the Committee*, pg. 260.
8   Mills, pg. 14.
9   Campbell, Charles C., *Hell Exploded. An Exposition of Barbarous Cruelty and Prison Horrors*, pg. 19.
10 *Report of the Penitentiary Investigating Committee including All Exhibits and Testimony Taken by the Committee, Published by Order of the House of Representatives, August 1910*, pg. 18.
11 Mills, pg. 13.
12 Simmons, Lee, *Assignment Huntsville*, pg. ix.
13 Ibid., pg. x.
14 Ibid.

Chapter Six

(1889-1904)

The Man Who Fought the Brutality and Oppression of the Ring in the State of Texas for Eighteen Years and Won

The Texas Prison Memoir of Henry Tomlin

I remember, too, a crazy boy, May Selmer by name, from Corsicana, sent up for arson. I have known Ezell to beat this boy with a bed slat until he finally got through the door of his cell and ran out in the yard with only a shirt on and wildly called for help. I have known the guards to throw pans of water on him, off and on through the night. I have known them to take his bedding away from him at night and leave him to sleep on the bare cement floor. I have known them to dip an old soup pan into a box of air-slaked lime and throw panful after panful over him, while he was in the back part of his cell, and not allowed even a drink of water all night long. Night after night he has begged me for water.

Henry Tomlin was an inmate who, for sixteen years, taunted, defied, and challenged the guards and other inmates at the Rusk penitentiary. The guards, in return, beat him, isolated him in the "dark cell," starved him, and left him a crippled and bitter man.

Tomlin was finally released from prison in 1904 and two years later vented his anger and frustration at the Texas prison system in a self-published memoir. While most ex-inmate narratives tended to be relatively short histories of personal prison experiences, Tomlin's finished product was a 272-page indictment including what appear to be poorly staged reenactment photographs of prison torture, abuse, and even murder.

That personal narrative, which he published as *Henry Tomlin, the man who fought the brutality and oppression of the ring in the state of Texas for eighteen years and won. Or The story of how men traffic in the liberties and lives of their fellow men,* gives an extremely biased but also very descriptive account of the Texas prison system from 1889 to 1904.

The title suggests Tomlin saw himself in the role of abused and tormented martyr in this account of his sixteen years incarcerated inside the Texas prison system (he included two years pretrial and appellate jail time in the title).

Henry Tomlin was charged with, tried for, and convicted of rape in 1888. At that time in Texas prisons, rapists were labeled as "rape fiends" and held in extreme contempt by the guards and other inmates. Much like child molesters in prisons today, rapists in the 1800s were singled out for punishment and retaliation.

That fact might explain some of the institutional adjustment problems Tomlin experienced throughout those sixteen years, but another major problem was his self-serving and condescending attitude toward the guards and other inmates.

In *Henry Tomlin, the man who…* Tomlin makes a continuous series of allegations against what he sees as "subhuman prison guards and ignorant inmates"—complete with racial, ancestral, and personal slurs. His narrative, not surprisingly, is one of personal hardship and punishment while in prison.

Tomlin, who insisted the remainder of his life that he was innocent of the rape charge, emerged from the Texas prison system in 1904 determined to plead his innocence publicly and issue a wholesale "indictment" of the penitentiary for his "unjust" incarceration.

His sense of self-importance is apparent in the introduction of his memoir when he characterizes himself as having undergone more brutal treatment than any other man in the world.

His prison experiences were abusive in nature, to the extreme, but the accounts of too many other inmates serving in the work crews, coal mines, and cotton fields during the convict lease period years suggest his claim was made in ignorance about the conditions of those thousands of leased convicts in the late 1800s.

In *Henry Tomlin, the man who…*, after a prolonged introduction designed to establish his innocence of the rape charges, he describes his conviction at Waxahachie, in Ellis County, on March 28, 1888. He was transferred to Rusk penitentiary on January 2, 1889.

Like other narratives of this period, Tomlin professes to have published his prison story as a warning to young people contemplating a life of crime. Even here, however, he mixes his warning with a protestation of his innocence:

> I hope that my experience will be a warning to the
> youth of the land and that they, by a manly, upright

course, may avoid the harsh clutches of the law; for if an innocent man had to undergo such torture, what must be the condition of a willfully guilty one?

Henry Tomlin developed his narrative of the Texas prison system around his claim to have never been forced to work while in the penitentiary. "I am the only man ever known to have been in prison for nearly sixteen years that the prison officials could not force, nor by them be made to work" he boasts.

It was his desire to promote himself as "the convict who would not work" that caused most of his problems in prison. Because of his refusal to follow orders, he spent most of his time in a solitary cell.

His problems began almost immediately after his arrival at Rusk in January 1889. Upon arrival, he and several other new inmates were sent to the mess hall and given their first food in nearly two days. Under strict orders not to talk at the table, he made jokes about the food that almost resulted in the entire group of inmates being sent to the dark cell, a punishment later referred to as "solitary confinement." In 1889 the "dark cell" had the added misery of being painted black inside— making it pitch dark.

Tomlin, a very opinionated and bigoted man, also had issues with being imprisoned with black and Mexican inmates at Rusk. While Texas prisons were strictly segregated in the 1800s, the main units at Huntsville and Rusk did house inmates of all races.

Immediately upon arrival at Rusk, Tomlin began having problems with other convicts. One of the things that disturbed him most was the fact that he was in the company of black inmates who thought they were the social equals of white convicts.

Tomlin pursues this theme in depth in *Henry Tomlin, the man who...*, even to the point of suggesting that many Negroes looked forward to going to prison and "fulfilling their wildest dreams of social equality."

> There never was more honor bestowed upon a negro than when a District Judge passes sentence upon him and sends him to the penitentiary. Here he is taught to read and write and placed on equality with the white man.
>
> When the sentence to the penitentiary is passed on him by the District Judge, he feels at once that he is elevated to a much higher position than ever could or would be his portion on earth, and his imprudence is aroused to an unbearable extent.

Tomlin continued, "It is a hard matter for a high-strung white man to retain his self-respect and keep his good time while he is forced to mix and mingle with them."

Prison administration has always been a strictly regimented system, perhaps even more so than the military. Each level of prison administration has official duties specified, and officers tend to be very protective of what they see as their responsibilities.

Tomlin almost immediately proved himself to be a master at playing one officer against another, although the end result was almost always that both officers would take their anger out on him in some retaliatory form.

His earliest target for this "undermining of authority" was a captain named "Ezell." Inmates at Rusk generally despised this Captain Ezell, evidenced by stories of brutality attributed to him in other narratives of this period.

Tomlin antagonized Ezell by constantly going over his head to undermine his authority, especially in front of the other inmates. Then, when he later found himself at the mercy of that same captain, Tomlin always claimed he was being singled out for retaliation.

One example occurred early in Tomlin's sentence at Rusk: On Sundays, inmates were allowed to write one letter to family or friends on the outside at state expense. Inmates with good behavior could write a second letter, but the convict had to pay the postage himself. One particular Sunday, Tomlin wrote three letters and was denied permission by Captain Ezell to mail the third letter since it was against the rules.

Tomlin's response was to contact the assistant superintendent of the prison who, unaware of Ezell's denial, allowed Tomlin to mail the third letter. When confronted by Ezell, Tomlin told him, "I knew that Captain Douglas was the assistant superintendent and ought to be running that place."

Not surprisingly, he found himself transferred the next day from a relatively good job assignment as a planer in the woodshop to a dreaded work assignment in the iron foundry. Tomlin, still not realizing the mistake he was making, immediately demanded to see the prison doctor and proceeded to once again go behind Captain Ezell's back to the assistant superintendent in an attempt to get a medial exemption from the foundry.

As was almost always the case, his "game" backfired and the captain was backed by the higher prison administration. Tomlin, smoldering in indignation, claims that he worked in the prison foundry for fifteen days and on January 23, 1889, the injustice of the job assignment became too much to bear and he began refusing to turn out for work.

"I told the officials that I had quit work and that 'I did not owe the State anything, and that being the case I would not pay it anything.' This was my motto from then until my release from prison," he later wrote.

Tomlin claims that date, January 23, 1889, marked the beginning of his years of torture by Captain Ezell.

In the 1800s blister plasters were made of Spanish fly shells, ground up and made into a paste. Application of this paste was used to raise blisters, and much like the early medical practice of "leeching" blood from patients, these Spanish fly blister plasters were applied to affected skin areas. The skin would become very irritated and blistered, and blood would be sucked to the surface in what was a very painful and dreaded medical procedure at the time.

Tomlin claims Captain Ezell ordered him tied down in his cell and another inmate ordered to apply the paste to raise blisters all over his back. Then, after he'd been allowed to suffer long enough, Ezell would order other inmates to probe the blisters and apply irritants such as iodine or mustard oils into the raw areas to increase the pain.

If this treatment hadn't brought home the reality of his imprisonment to Tomlin, the offended captain then had him thrown naked into a cell that had been stripped of everything except water and slop buckets. For fifty-seven days, he claims, he was forced to sleep on a bare cement floor and was fed only a small piece of bread measuring about three inches by three inches and one inch thick, and only three times a day.

It would be impossible to verify or dispute Tomlin's claims of physical torture at Rusk. Certainly other accounts from inmates during that period collaborate many of his claims. The inspector of the Texas state penitentiary had himself thirteen years earlier reported gross physical abuses within the system that resemble the treatment Tomlin alleges.[1]

During this period of personal torture, Tomlin also claims he had his hands cuffed together and was hung from the ceiling of his cell in a manner that caused his legs to give out and leave him swinging from his wrists.

Other times, he alleges, he was taken out of his cell, a rope tied around his ankles and wrists, and the guards would "stretch" him out before beating him unconscious. "I underwent every sepcies [*sic*] of punishment and torture known, and which are entirely too numerous to mention," he claims.

In *Henry Tomlin, the man who...*, he offers a staged photograph of himself dressed in striped prison clothes and hanging by his wrists. Other punishments during this period, he claims, included torture by other inmates and strapping. He also offers staged photographs of these activities as illustration.

After fifty-seven days lying on a cement floor, he alleges, the prison surgeon ordered him removed to the hospital.

> I was confined for four months without shave, haircut or change of clothes, and I never had a bath for eight months and seven days. Then I was taken to the hospital. When the fresh air struck me I fainted and my fellow convicts carried me into the first ward and put me on a bed. The convict doctor had the windows lowered and the draft regulated, until I could get used to it. He sat on the side of the bed and worked with me until I became conscious, then ordered the windows and doors opened gradually, until I could stand it.

Then, he claims, he remained in the hospital until April 1890 when he was discharged so physically maimed that he required crutches to walk. Immediately upon release from the hospital, he was sent back to the yard on crutches and told to report to Captain Ezell.

Tomlin still refused to do any work. He claims the guards conspired to fabricate false charges against him and managed to have him locked in the "dark cell" and again beaten unmercifully.

After his release from the dark cell, Captain Ezell had him reassigned to his old living quarters located on the third tier. Because of his crutches, he could almost never leave his cell, and the location made it nearly impossible for him to move around the unit to eat, get medical attention, or even receive mail.

Shortly before Christmas of 1890, Governor Hogg visited the prison at Rusk accompanied by members of the Texas newspaper media. Tomlin, anxious to approach the governor with a long list of grievances against the prison system and Captain Ezell, was surprised when the officer had him transferred back into the hospital where he was isolated and denied the opportunity to speak with the governor.

Throughout his narrative, Tomlin never seemed to understand the consequences of his undermining Ezell's authority.

Although he claims to have "undergone more brutal treatment than any other man in the world and lived over it," he also acknowledges that he was not the only convict to be singled out for punishment by Ezell and the other prison authorities.

According to the narrative, a Mexican who had lost both feet was dying of consumption and gangrene, was denied medical attention, and eventually died a painful death in the winter of 1894.

The crazy boy from Corsicana was tormented by beatings, had water and air-slaked lime thrown on him in his cell, and was denied food and drinking water. Eventually, according to Tomlin, the young man survived to discharge Rusk only to later die as a raving maniac in the Corsicana jail.

An "old crazy Negro" was nearly beaten to death for "feigning insanity" and was then housed with the truly crazy inmates until he did go insane himself.

While Tomlin was locked up as an inmate, it would have been impossible for him to provide documentation or verification of these events. After his release from prison, he still had no verifiable proof other than the collaboration of other ex-convicts. What he provided in *Henry Tomlin, the man who…* was a series of photographs, obviously staged, to illustrate his allegations.

One illustration shows an inmate in clean, starched, prisoner clothing lying dead over a crosscut saw in an unnamed field as guards and other inmates look on. Since Tomlin never worked on a wood crew in the field (or any other prison job anywere), he may not have realized that those who did often worked months without bathing or laundering and sometimes went years without changes of clothing. This particular illustration also shows the field guards dressed in suits with ties and wearing bowler hats—an image refuted by every other narrative of that period.

That particular illustration, however, did list the dead inmate's name: a convict named "Moseley." Another narrative, written by a former inmate at Rusk, would also allege this inmate named Moseley had died while working at a crosscut saw and been left lying in the field all day in that position.

Henry Tomlin, the man who fought the brutality and oppression of the ring in the state of Texas for eighteen years and won Or The story of how men traffic in the liberties and lives of their fellow men is basically a book of allegations and personal indictments against the Texas prison system. And while much of what Tomlin alleged would later be substantiated in official prison audit reports and independent newspaper accounts, *Henry Tomlin, the man who…* also differs radically from similar accounts given by other convicts during this period.

Tomlin is referred to in another narrative of that time period published by a former prisoner named Charles Campbell. In his memoir *Hell Exploded*, Campbell referred to Tomlin's extended punishment and isolation but in a much different perspective than *Henry Tomlin, the man who….*

Campbell, who was serving time at Rusk during this same period, refers to Henry *Tumlin*, of Waxahachie, who sprained his back in the foundry and could not lift. As a result, Campbell asserts, Tomlin was lashed thirty-nine times and told to return to work. Tomlin, according to Campbell's account, "begged and plead [*sic*] with them to believe and spare him, promising to work all the harder when he got well. He could not obey the command to resume work because he was absolutely unable to walk."[2]

This account is far different from Tomlin's own claim "I told the officials that I had quit work and that I did not owe the State anything, and that being the case I would not pay it anything. This was my motto from then until my release from prison."

Campbell does describe Tomlin's continued physical abuse and extended isolation in the dark cell. It is impossible to tell exactly why the two versions differed so radically.

Tomlin claims the treatment he received at the hands of Captain Ezell while at Rusk left him crippled and partially paralyzed. Despite his maiming injuries, Tomlin states, this brutal and sadistic treatment would continue until his release from the penitentiary in 1904.

After sixteen years of imprisonment, including over fourteen at Rusk penitentiary, Henry Tomlin received a pardon from Governor Lanham.

By 1904 Tomlin had become so bitter and filled with hatred for the system that he ignored the true meaning of the document and attempted to use the pardon as proof of his innocence with regards to the rape charges and to validate his claims of "false imprisonment" by the state of Texas.

A copy of the pardon is included in *Henry Tomlin, the man who fought the brutality and oppression of the ring in the state of Texas for eighteen years and won Or The story of how men traffic in the liberties and lives of their fellow men.*

The document Tomlin submits does recognize that in 1904 he was a partially paralyzed inmate in the state prison system. But it also clearly states that the pardon was issued "waiving the question of the applicant's guilt or innocence." While Tomlin exhibited the pardon as proof of his innocence, in reality it only recognized his grave medical condition and ignored the issue of his guilt.

Henry Tomlin almost certainly was a man with few friends and a person with the ability and desire to alienate almost everyone with whom he came in contact. His tirades against the other inmates, whom he referred to as "brutes" and "flunkies," his deep-seated racial bigotry, and his intentional alienation of the guards who controlled him indicate he was a prisoner who sought out confrontation and retaliation.

Even his personal life after parole was marked with discord and confrontation: Immediately upon his returning to Waxahachie from Rusk, his wife filed for divorce.

Henry Tomlin, the man who fought the brutality and oppression of the ring in the state of Texas for eighteen years and won ... provides an interesting but mostly unsubstantiated view of the conditions inside Rusk penitentiary in the final years of the nineteenth century. His refusal to abandon his anger and self-righteousness makes its accuracy somewhat suspect.

---

1   *Report of the Inspector, office of the Inspector, Texas State Penitentiary, Huntsville Texas, January 31, 1876*, pp. 14-16.
2   Campbell, Charles C., *Hell Exploded*, pg. 20.

Chapter Seven

Women in Chains

It sounds like a poorly written script for a "B Grade" 1960s sexploitation movie: Female prisoners being tied by the hands, stripped, and whipped in front of other inmates and guards; midnight visits to the women's barracks by male guards for personal pleasure; offers of parole recommendations for sexual favors; women serving long sentences becoming pregnant, and even a baby born in the dirt between two rows of cotton while guards look on.

But the script was not a Hollywood narrative; it was taken directly from the *Report of the Penitentiary Investigating Committee including All Exhibits and Testimony Taken by the Committee,* published by the Texas House of Representatives in 1910.

During a period when newspapers were still avoiding the word "rape" in print, these revelations by the legislature were received in Texas with indignation and repulsion by individual citizens, religious and civic groups, and political officials.

Few passages in the massive 1910 legislative report had such devastating impact with regard to the state prison system and convict lease system as did the descriptions of the female prisoners isolated on the remote Eastham Camp #2.

A year and a half earlier, *San Antonio Express* reporter George Waverly Briggs had alerted the Texas public to the conditions of the women convicts in a sensational but largely undocumented column.[1] Briggs' columns are generally

This is how Charles Favor portrayed female inmates in 1900. Just how he would have had access to this information on a female unit is not explained, but these contented and smiling women portray a prison scene far different from the 1910 legislative report citing female prisoners being subjected to whippings, strip searches, and sexual demands by male guards. It is far different from the documented report of a female prisoner giving birth between two cotton rows while male guards watched. Favor, Charles A., *Twenty-Two Months in the Texas Penitentiary* (Corsicana, TX: Democrat Print, 1900).

credited with leading to the call for the investigation by the Texas legislature.

But women had been incarcerated in the Texas prison system for a half-century by the time Briggs and the legislature made their revelations. It is believed the first woman convict to be processed into the Texas prison system was Elizabeth Huffman, sentenced to one year in 1854 for the killing of a child.

By 1892 Charles Favor was observing in Huntsville, "It is a sad sight to see women donned in stripes. There are but a few white women, the balance being Negresses. These women attend the garden and do such work with the needle as comes up. There is a great deal of prison talk that would sound romantic and shameful concerning this department of the Penitentiaries." [2]

Sixteen years later Briggs would write in his column, "At this time there are confined sixty-seven of the State's weak, unfortunate women at the Eastham Farm. For the variable female population of sixty to one hundred convicts in the Texas prison there is not an official matron. There is not a member of their sex to attend to their needs and wants; there is not a woman of sympathetic mien and heart to minister to their minds diseased; there is not a woman of delicate sensibilities and modest demeanor to perform the bodily examinations which the law requires to be made of each prisoner incarcerated...."

Women, like the men in the convict lease system, were considered by prison officials to be no more than animals, according to Briggs. "They are thieves, liars, perverts and murderesses, in the eyes of the administration, upon whom it were a waste of time and money to bestow the least reforming influence, and therefore, like 'dumb, driven cattle,' they are fed, watered and groomed to the end...."

But few allegations in Briggs' column had the impact with the Texas public as did the report that three babies also lived on the Eastham Camp #2:

> There are three babies at this farm. They sleep and eat with their mothers in the prison building and constitute one of the few enlivening and loveable integers of this forlorn habitation. One of them...was born on the Bowden farm, eight miles from Huntsville, whence this colony was moved last year. She is the child of Cora Morgan, a coal-black life-time prisoner who has been in the penitentiary seven years. The child is about two years of age...This child has a younger half-sister,

Prisoner's barracks and guards at Camp 2 of the Eastham Prison Farm located near Weldon, Texas (Circa: 1914). It was here that a San Antonio newspaper reporter earlier had disclosed women prisoners were being housed and worked in the fields. Photo courtesy of Robert H. Russell and the Texas Prison Museum, Huntsville, Texas.

a baby in arms, which is of decidedly full-blooded African lineage. The other child in the prison is ten months of age; its mother has been in the penitentiary, according to her statement, nearly two years.[3]

But if Briggs' allegations weren't damning enough, he also reported yet another incident of a pregnant female convict being forced to report to a "hoe squad" in the field only to give birth to a baby in the dirt between two cotton rows:

On the women's farm, a year ago last spring, a child was born in the field, sans attention, medical care or decency. Hours afterward, according to the statement of a witness, the sand of the cotton field still adhered to and lacerated its tender little body, as it writhed in the first activities of life....

On the morning of the child's birth the prison mates of its mother protested against her being sent to the field...The woman was ordered to the field to hoe her row with her companions.

Briggs concluded his column with the observation that the mistreatment of the women appeared to be conducted with the tacit approval of prison officials in Huntsville:

Why does it [Texas] continue to maintain the female convicts in an isolated farm twenty miles from the penitentiary headquarters, accessible only by a rugged road through the bottom lands of the Trinity River? As applicable to the women convicts the plan of the Texas Penitentiary is not only inhumane and mercenary, but it is unholy. Brutalities have occurred in the past and under the present administration, yet the women are taken deeper into the woods and further away from the observation of the higher officers. On its face it looks as if the powers are placing a premium on the infraction of rules by affording the offender a means of concealment.

It appears Briggs' conclusion directly influenced the legislative investigating committee when it reported in 1910:

The female convicts of the State are located at Eastham camp No. 2, some twenty-three miles from Huntsville, there being about sixty-seven Negro women, three whites and one Mexican at the time of the committee's visit there. The Negro women are employed in the fields in the cultivation of corn, cotton, etc., the white women and the Mexican women being employed at light work about the place. The Negroes occupy a building to themselves. The entire force is under the supervision of men only. Evidence of disgraceful conduct on the part of former employees, and two now in the service, was presented to the committee, which evidence is merely referred to, as the same is too shocking and repulsive to put in this report.[4]

The report then went on to recommend that all female convicts be placed upon a farm, segregated from male convicts, owned by the state and not leased out on isolated work camps. It was also recommended that the sergeant in charge of such farm be a married man and that his family should live there with him.

Significantly, the committee also demanded that a matron be employed on the female convict farm with the authority to look after the physical welfare and wants of the women, and to determine whether or not the physical condition of the females was such that they are able to perform manual labor.

With regards to the living conditions of the female convicts, the committee also demanded that an assistant matron be employed to directly supervise the women in the barracks at night and that all male guards assigned to the women's farm be married men living with their families.[5]

Briggs' column and the 1910 committee report led to the abolition of the convict lease system and unquestionably resulted in far more favorable conditions for the women serving time in the Texas prison system.

By 1925 Milt Good recalled, "The women prisoners at Goree are engaged mostly in sewing on these white uniforms."[6]

The placing of women in chains and behind cell bars has always been problematic for Texas society. Even today the incarceration of females leads to charges of misconduct on the part of male guards.[7]

But even the most cynical critic of Texas prisons today would have to admit that conditions for female prisoners have improved since the degrading and "unholy" days of the convict lease system.

1   "Treatment of These Women is Inhuman," *San Antonio Express*, December 13, 1908.
2   Favor, Charles A., *Twenty-Two Months in the Texas Penitentiary*, pg. 119.
3   *San Antonio Express*, December 13, 1908.
4   *Report of the Penitentiary Investigating Committee including All Exhibits and Testimony Taken by the Committee, Published by Order of the House of Representatives, August 1910.*, pg. 14.
5   Ibid., pg. 16.
6   Good, Milt, *Twelve Years in a Texas Prison*, pg. 24.
7   "Inmate Abuse Covered Up, Ex-Guard Says in Lawsuit," *Houston Chronicle*, September 28, 1999, Sect. A., pg. 17.

Chapter Eight

"Necking" on the Way to Prison

Transportation of convicted felons who are often dangerous and desperate men has always been a headache for prison authorities. The use of chains probably dates back to the earliest days of the British convict ships arriving at colonial ports in the New World and continues even today. The methods, however, have changed considerably over the years.

From the first arrival at the new Texas prison in Huntsville in 1849, it is certain that chains played a part in his transfer from the county jail location of his conviction.

Initially, chained inmates were taken to Huntsville sitting in the backs of wagons—often open and exposed to the elements and the stares of the townspeople with whom they came into contact on the journey. Later, trains were used to transport prisoners from their county jails.

In 1922 the Texas prison system adopted the new motorized transportation when Bud Russell modified an oversized flatbed truck with a frame of boilerplate and heavy wire mesh. The back was essentially a heavy-gauge metal cage with one entrance, consisting of two narrow double doors, at the rear on the driver side.

But even these security measures did not eliminate the need to keep the convicts in chains during transportation. Russell's truck had a steel bar running down the center onto which the inmate's chains were attached while transporting. As a result, Russell's truck became known as a "chain bus," a term still used today describing the white busses transporting Texas prisoners to prison or from unit to unit.

Of all the security techniques developed by Texas prison officials during the 1800s and first half of the twentieth century, the "necking," or use of steel neck collars attached to chains, seems to have been one of the most humiliating tools used by prison authorities.

In the 1800s, before the days of radio and television, the county courthouse was often the social center of the community and even sometimes for the whole county. Today at many rural Texas courthouses, benches are placed outside the entrances to the building, and throughout the day retired men sit and visit with their neighbors.

But in the 1800s the courthouse often also provided the primary news stories locally. When a felony trial was conducted, citizens from throughout the county would often pack the courtroom or follow the proceedings closely from outside. When a conviction was obtained, the results were often front-page banner headline newspaper news.

Likewise, when prison officials arrived at the county jails to take charge of the newly convicted prisoners, that transfer of custody was often also met with interest—at times even with festivities. As the convicts were placed in wagons or marched through town wearing neck chains to the train station, crowds would often gather, cheering or taunting the men on their way to prison.

But the event was not always festive. The period following the Civil War also marked an era in Texas history that featured lynching and vigilante justice. Prisoners convicted of particularly heinous crimes were often pulled from their cells by mobs and hung from courthouse tree branches.

So that brief, vulnerable period in which they were removed from jail for transport to prison also was a time of great tension for many prisoners as they were paraded through the crowds of citizens to start their journey to Huntsville or Rusk.

From the prison officer's point of view, transport is also one of the riskiest times with regards to escape attempts, especially when a newly convicted prisoner is facing a long sentence.

So the oldest technique remained the best technique—chain the men together with heavy chains attached to steel collars around their necks. It was a technique used into the 1950s in Texas prisons. It was also the technique that prisoners had detested for at least a century before.

This undated photograph shows inmates at an undisclosed prison unit being "necked." The use of neck chains was particularly hated as indicated by the expressions on the faces of these four inmates. Brazoria County Historical Museum Photograph Collection

With regards to the personal narratives, one of the very earliest was that of Andrew George in 1885 when he wrote, "…on the 20th of August was chained round the neck to a man by the name of Sharpe, and taken to Huntsville, Texas State prison.…"[1]

The humiliation factor was also resented, and the public parading of "necked" prisoners was recalled with shame by several ex-convicts who wrote of their experiences. In their eyes, the "necking" factor reduced them to the status of animals when done in public.

In 1898 J.S. Calvin wrote,

About 10 o'clock in the morning the transfer agent put in his appearance and we were ordered out of our cells and lined up two and two like oxen and necked together with chains around our necks with a connecting chain about two feet long between each two and then they were all strung together on one long chain like a team of several yoke of cattle…It seemed the whole town and a good part of the county knew that we were to be transferred that day for when we marched out of the jail I thought that Barnum's circus must be in town from the looks of the crowd. And when we got to the depot the train was about thirty minutes late and we was compelled to stand out on the platform where we were exposed to the glare of the July sun and the glare of the crowd as they walked around and gazed as though we were a lot of lions and tigers or some other strange beasts, instead of a lot of human beings. It was the same thing all along the line for it seemed to us that there was either a picnic or a circus at every station that we passed and they appeared to be aware of our presence long before the train would arrive. For as soon as the train would pull into the station it would be covered by crowds of curious spectators eager to get a glimpse at the great curiosity and ask questions....[2]

Also in the 1890s, Charles Campbell, with his use of sarcastic and presumptuous prose, described the crowd of people watching him leave for prison: "Soon after the court wound up at Kaufman, the State contractor put in his appearance with his endless chain system, and soon we all had substantial ornaments around our necks. On the way to the depot I extemporized a little farewell address to the many onlookers entitled "The Ties that Bind us."

Free lunch fiends and human velocipedes: You are doubtless aware that there are a great many different kinds of ties—cross-ties, neckties, matrimonial ties and family ties. You now behold one of the closest ties that has ever been your privilege to look upon. We are bound together with bonds of steel lest that by some means this union might be broken, and we accidentally drift apart. We would be heartless, indeed, were we to fail to appreciate your thoughtful solicitude. It causes the bile to bile in our inactive liver regions and our tongues to lay still under their coats and vests with unspeakable emotion when we consider what precautionary methods you employ to keep us among you.[3]

By 1910 little had changed. Bill Mills would later recall: "So they brought fourteen of us into the jail office and lined us up like oxen, two and two. They put a short chain from neck to neck of each couple, then the end of a long chain was locked to a ring in the middle of the chain of the front rank. It extended backward through the middle of each chain to the back pair. So you see it really looked like seven yoke of oxen."[4]

For many of the earliest narratives, this "necking" event took place in the years immediately after the Civil War and Reconstruction when Texas had entered into a period of extreme segregation of the races.

While the convict lease camps tended to be organized along strictly segregated lines with regards to race, the main units at Huntsville and Rusk were surprisingly integregated in the 1800s. Several of the writers during that period objected to being imprisoned around black inmates.

Henry Tomlin was one of the most vocal, and wrote: "It is true that the Negroes occupy separate cells and are fed at separate tables...one of these burly brutes will push right in to show the social equality. If one should knock him down it is an infringement of the rules and the white man is punished accordingly. Now, doesn't it look as if the Negro should be restrained and kept on his own side?"[5]

Probably due to the costs and logistics related to transporting prisoners, the races were often placed together during the necking process probably to the chagrin of both groups, but certainly the white inmates.

In 1892 Charles Favor recalled of his transport: "At Tyler we picked up others whose fates were similar to our own, and we now numbered nineteen—black and white are chained together"[6] And six years later J.S. Calvin recorded, "the whites on one string and the Negroes on another."[7]

The necking process, once applied, remained until the inmates were safely delivered to the prison unit, no matter how far or long the journey. Especially after the arrival of train transportation in Texas, the trip would usually require no longer than two or three days. During that period the neck chains would remain on throughout the entire process, resulting in considerable discomfort.

This was the hated neck chain described by almost every inmate who later wrote accounts of their incarceration in the 1800s. Inmates would be lined up in a row, the neck chains attached, and another longer chain would be run through the large link on the end—forcing the inmate "chain gang" to march in lock-step to avoid choking each other.
Photo by Gary Brown, courtesy of the Texas Prison Museum

Favor wrote of his experience in 1892, "We were kept in the depot overnight. I could not sleep."[8] During that same period, Charles Campbell recalled:

> We arrived at Tyler bout 10 o'clock at night and had to lay on the cold, sandy floor without covering of any kind till morning, when we were loaded onto a frosty flat car and headed for the last division...After getting off the train we drilled up the railroad to prison a mile and a half from town...We were next passed through another gate, and were then inside the walls proper. They then marched us to the underkeeper's office, where the necklaces were taken off....[9]

"Necking" continued in Texas prisons well into the second half of the 1900s. In 1925 Milt Good reported, "The first stage of our journey was made by interurban train from Dallas to Corsicana. This was our first experience on 'The Chain.' The prisoners were shackled together in pairs by a chain that locked around the neck. This chain was then locked to a center or lead chain. Each prisoner soon learned that he must hold tightly to the lead chain to keep others from jerking it and hurting his neck with the smaller chain."[10]

Today Texas prisoners are no longer necked when being transported across state. Deemed "cruel and unusual" by the courts, prison officials have abandoned the practice and today use what are called "belly chains." Inmates being transported are chained around the waist and handcuffed with the cuffs being fastened to the waist chain so they cannot raise their hands above their belts. Assaultive inmates may also be cuffed around the ankles with their feet connected to a short chain as well.

The emphasis today is on security and safety, but for over a century, the Texas prison transportation process relied upon "necking" with its considerable discomfort and humiliation factors.

1   George, Andrew L., *The Texas Convict: Sketches of the Penitentiary, Convict Farms and Railroads, Together with Poems*, pg. 2.

2   Calvin, J.S., *Buried alive, or, A term in the Texas State Prison, 1898-1902: a chapter from real life*, pg. 27.

3   Campbell, Charles C., *Hell Exploded. An Exposition of Barbarous Cruelty and Prison Horrors*, pg. 12.

4   Mills, Bill, *25 Years Behind Prison Bars*, pp. 4-5.

5   Tomlin, Henry, *Henry Tomlin, the man who fought the brutality and oppression of the ring in the state of Texas for eighteen years and won. The story of how men traffic in the liberties and lives of their fellow men*, pp. 34-35.

6   Favor, Charles A., *Twenty-Two Months in the Texas Penitentiary*, pg. 18.

7   Calvin, pg. 27.

8   Favor, pg. 18.

9   Campbell, pp. 13-14.

10 Good, Milt, *Twelve Years in a Texas Prison*, pg. 22.

Chapter Nine

(1878-1894)

Sixteen Years at Huntsville

The Texas Prison Memoir of John Wesley Hardin

My sides and back were beaten into a jelly, and, still quivering and bleeding, they made me walk in the snow across to another building, where they placed me in a dark cell and threatened to starve me to death if I did not reveal the plot. I told them I would tell them nothing; that I meant to escape and would kill them in a minute if they stood in my way. They left me there for three days without anything to eat or drink, and on the fourth day I was carried to another cell in a high fever and unable to walk. I stayed there for thirty days.

The personal narratives published during the Texas convict lease period were the memoirs of men who were relatively unknown outside the communities from which they were tried and sentenced. The majority of stories were self-published— often printed on small presses with the author paying the costs of publication.

Distribution was usually also handled by the writer, either as an attempt to sell the stories or to use them to expose the prison system and describe their experiences inside it. As a result, most of these stories were never widely circulated.

One notable exception, however, was an autobiography published in 1896 by a man well known in Texas and a name recognized throughout the United States.

John Wesley Hardin was a legend, although one with a fading reputation, when he was shot from behind and killed in the Acme Saloon on August 19, 1895, in El Paso. Among the few possessions he left behind was a handwritten diary of his life that he had hoped to sell as a self-promoting autobiography.

The year after his death, his children did arrange for a Seguin publisher to print the manuscript but found there was little market for the book. Over the years, however, reprints have kept his version of his life on bookshelves and in libraries.

Despite the skepticism of many historians, *The Life of John Wesley Hardin As Written by Himself* has been, since its first publication, the primary source of information about the legendary gunfighter.

One area of particular interest in the book is Hardin's account of his time as an inmate in the Texas prison system. He spent sixteen years at Huntsville from 1878 through 1894.

John Wesley Hardin was the documented killer of many men by the time he was apprehended in Florida, extradited to Texas, tried for murder, convicted, and sentenced to twenty-five years in the penitentiary.

After his sentencing at Comanche, Texas, he was shackled to three other inmates and transported by wagon to Huntsville, encountering large crowds at every stop. He arrived at the prison on October 5, 1878.

By his own account, his reputation and status had no bearing on the way prison officials treated him once he entered the massive gates and was processed into the system. In a routine that continues today in Texas prisons, Hardin was stripped, given a shave and haircut, and a physical inventory of body markings recorded.

Hardin later wrote that he was given a breakfast of coffee, bacon, bread, and molasses that morning. Later during processing, the Bertillion officer recorded that he had dark hair, hazel eyes, a light complexion, and that his body markings revealed multiple wounds and scars.

He was then given a work assignment in the wheelwright shop where he quickly put the bits, chisels, and other tools to work in tunneling out of the prison. With surprising candor, Hardin later wrote of his own naiveté while incarcerated.

Naiveté in that he enlisted the cooperation and help of some seventy-five other inmates in his escape plan. He would later recall, "I knew there were a heap of Judases and Benedict Arnolds in the world and had had a lifelong experience with the meaning of the word treachery. I believed, however, that in jail even a coward was a brave man, so I went to work to plan my escape."[1]

The plan started around November 1, 1878, only three weeks after his arrival, and was completed around November 20. According to Hardin, all that was left was to burst through the pine wood floor of the armory while the unarmed guards were eating supper and execute the escape plan. Not surprisingly, given the number of people involved, he was reported to the officials and the plan was thwarted before he could escape.

Hardin and nine other convicts were seized. Hardin was placed in the dark cell for fifteen days on a bread and water diet and then released. As was common with long-term convicts with escape records, he had a ball and chain forged onto his ankle by the prison blacksmith. The heavy steel ball chained to his ankle would remain after his release from the dark cell.

Texas prison officials were obviously unimpressed with Hardin's reputation or celebrity status prior to being sentenced to Huntsville because the ball and chain were reserved for incorrigible inmates or high escape risks.

When he was released back into the general inmate population, he was celled with a "turnkey," another inmate given special privileges in return for manning the cellblock doors and helping control the movement of the other inmates through the use of a gate key.

Despite the fact that his new cellmate was one of the inmates he had enlisted in the tunneling escape plan and had received a preferential job rather than the dark cell afterwards, Hardin still did not figure out that he was being set up, or that he was still the tool of the "Judases and Benedict Arnolds" of the Texas state prison system.

He immediately enlisted this cellmate to begin duplicating keys to other cells, riot gates, and even the prison exits. He even obtained a key that allowed him to remove the ball-and-chain shackles at night and began planning another escape for the evening of December 26. This was another elaborate plan involving a mass release of inmates and the use of two pistols that had been smuggled into the prison.

The prison authorities again apprehended him before the plan could be put into action, and this time they were determined to stop his escape attempts for good. "That evening I was suddenly arrested and locked up. They searched me, found my keys and also the bolt in my shackles; in short, my cell mate had betrayed me and the game was up" he later recorded.[2]

That night about twenty prison guards entered his cell and forcibly tied ropes to his hands and feet. Then, forcing him face down on the floor, the ropes were stretched out and he was held while another officer gave him the maximum thirty-nine lashes with the bat.

Hardin later wrote in his autobiography, "He began to whip my naked body with this instrument. They were now flogging me and every lick left the imprint of every lash…I heard one of them say, 'Don't hit him in the same place so often.' At last the superintendent said, 'That will do,' after they had hit me thirty-nine lashes, the limit."[3]

On the first of February, he was assigned to work in the prison carpentry shop but claims he successfully used his flogging injuries to avoid work most of the time. By June 1879 he had been transferred to the boot and shoe shop "at my own solicitation and soon became one of the best fitters and cutters they ever had."

This period was not without incident, however, and early in 1880 prison documents indicate he was one of four inmates captured trying to escape again. This time, no longer trusting the other convicts who had always betrayed him, Hardin had relied on one other inmate and had concentrated on bribing a guard. But again, his accomplice betrayed him and he was thrown into solitary and flogged, although by his own account "not so cruelly as before."

Hardin would also claim he was strapped a third time, "for an imaginary crime," as a scare tactic. In another incident, he claims to have participated in a plan to take officers hostage in an escape and was offered a pistol at the time of the attempt and refused it. As a result, he states, he "drew out of it" and stood by as the escapees were arrested and later whipped.

In the fall of 1883 an old shotgun wound in his side and stomach abscessed. He later claimed that prison officials "made fun of me and treated me cruelly" while refusing him a hospital bed. In part due to his suffering, but also in response to his lack of treatment, Hardin lay in his cell for eight months recuperating. Finally prison officials tired of his refusal to go to work and put him on a bread and water diet until he agreed to return to his job.

He was assigned to the tailor shop making quilts. It is difficult to visualize the man once considered the most dangerous gunslinger in the West at a quilting frame in the Texas prison shop, but it appears to have been a job assignment that was agreeable to both the prison system and Wes Hardin.

Despite his widespread reputation, especially throughout Texas, surprisingly few other narratives written during the period he was at Huntsville mention him.

Andrew L. George, in *The Texas Convict*, wrote in 1885 that after processing into Huntsville, he was taken to the third floor of the factory and issued a job in the shoe shop. Going up to the shoe shop on the second floor, he recalls he saw the "legendary gunslinger John Wesley Hardin" at work in the tailor shop.[4] George, however, gives no specifics and doesn't mention Hardin again.

Another lease period inmate named A.J. Walker would also later write:

> I occupied a cell next to him when I first came here
> …He had about six years of the sentence served when
> I came here and was working in the shoe shop. He told
> me about having failed twice in an attempt to escape.
> He often spoke of his wife and two children and said
> his wife remained true to him up to her death. She
> died shortly before his time expired. The last six years
> of his sentence he worked in the taylor [*sic*] shop and
> during his leisure moments he studied law.[5]

By 1885 Hardin had begun another well-orchestrated plan to get out of prison, only this time his efforts didn't involve escape attempts and more significantly, didn't involve the other inmates. This time he was determined to "beat the system" through a program of self-improvement and cooperation with prison officials.

From 1880 through 1882 he participated as the president of an inmate debating society at Huntsville, at one point writing to his wife that he had championed the cause of women's rights in a recent debate.

The "deadliest gun in the West" had begun to show a more sensitive and intellectual side to a personality many law enforcement officers still felt held no conscience.

Continuing to pursue his new image, Hardin became the superintendent of the inmate Sunday school class and with his Bible in hand, taught and gave sermons to the Huntsville inmates.

On August 26, 1885, he wrote the assistant warden a letter begging for medical attention. Probably in large part due to his change in attitude and behavior, his request was approved by the prison administration and he began receiving at least some level of treatment; as a result, his health slowly improved.

Also in 1885 he first approached the prison superintendent, Thomas Goree, for advice regarding a course of reading to prepare to take a law exam and qualify as a lawyer in Texas. Goree referred his letter to a local Huntsville attorney who, in turn, suggested a program of study. Somehow Hardin obtained the necessary law books and began preparing to become an attorney.

The dreaded and feared gunfighter of years earlier was now defending women's rights, teaching Sunday school, delivering sermons, and preparing to become an agent of the judicial system.

His correspondence with outside officials picked up, and in 1888 he wrote the assistant superintendent of the prison system a letter requesting a release date. The answer was not encouraging: "You continue to behave yourself, and you will go out at the proper time."

The following year, possibly in an attempt to test his developing law skills, he wrote the Texas legislature suggesting a number of prison reforms.

On a more personal approach he also wrote various legislators, campaigning for changes in the sentencing laws while also promoting his appeal for an early pardon or parole.

On January 1, 1893, he submitted another request for a pardon to Governor Hogg. Citing from his law books, he again claimed his innocence of the murder charges against him and presented a detailed and extensive rationale for requesting a pardon.

He also encouraged a campaign of letter writing by his friends outside of prison. Even after many years out of the public's awareness, he still had numerous friends and supporters.

In 1894 his personal appeals, legal petitions, letters of support, and even letters of recommendation from prison officials resulted in the issuance of the pardon he so badly wanted. On February 17, 1894, John Wesley Hardin walked out of the Huntsville prison a free man. He had spent fifteen years, eight months, and twelve days behind prison bars.

Hardin left Huntsville with all the appearances of a reformed man. And the early weeks of his freedom indicate he tried to become a legitimate lawyer. He set up an office briefly in Gonzales, Texas, and even had business cards printed up.

His old habits quickly returned, however, and he went through a period of problems with women, gamblers, outlaws, and law officials. Within eighteen months of his discharge from Huntsville, he was dead—shot from behind in very questionable circumstances while gambling in an El Paso saloon.

As his family sorted through the few possessions he left behind in El Paso after his death, the handwritten copy of *The Life of John Wesley Hardin As Written by Himself* was discovered and initially dismissed as worthless.

1   Hardin, John Wesley, *The Life of John Wesley Hardin As Written by Himself,* pg. 127.
2   Ibid., pg. 129.
3   Ibid., pg. 130.
4   George, Andrew L., *The Texas Convict*, pg. 11.
5   Hennessy, T.D., *The life of A.J. Walker,* pg. 62.

Chapter Ten

When the Sun Goes Down

The Rusk and Huntsville penitentiaries in the late 1800s were both well established and relatively secure prisons, attempting to utilize inmate labor through various industries. The narratives of that period indicate that inmates, both black and white, would do almost anything to be assigned to one of these units rather than be shipped out to one of the farms or, even worse, to one of the lease camps. If living conditions were less than desirable at Huntsville or Rusk, they bordered on inhumane and sadistic at the work camps and farms.

Away from the main prison units—and isolated from scrutiny by the public and prison administrators—convicts were housed in boxcars, railroad ditches, and even chained to trees at night. Even prior to the damning 1910 report by the legislature, county and small-town newspapers were editorializing about the brutal and inhumane conditions under which the convicts were living and working in the lease camps, particularly during construction of the Texas State Railroad in East Texas.

At Huntsville and Rusk the inmates were at least given wooden bunks in which to sleep at night—built two and sometimes three bunks high and usually covered by a corn shuck mattress (but not always).

In 1892 Charles Favor reported that at Rusk, "...there are three tiers of bunking quarters, and around each, at the bottom, is a plank twelve inches wide, called a run-a-round...."[1] He also recalls his first night at Rusk, when he was forced to share a wooden bunk with another convict who hadn't bathed for some time.

In the early 1900s J.L. Wilkinson wrote of stories being told by guards and convicts of the work camps outside the Rusk penitentiary. "The mosquitoes are so bad the convicts have to wear gunny sacks over their heads, and the guards go all day with a bunch of bushes in one hand with which to fight the mosquitoes and a gun in the other to keep the convicts going."

At night, Wilkinson challenges, "Imagine if you can, a room made foul by overcrowding with human beings, in the Texas river bottom, in the summer time, full of mosquitoes, with thousands of others to enter every time a screen or door is opened, and you will have a tolerably correct idea of the sleeping 'comforts' of the convict on the farm, week in and week out."[2]

Bill Mills, in 1915, described the conditions at Huntsville: "We had wooden frame bunks, one over the other, with hay mattresses and plenty of bed bugs to keep us company."[3]

One of the main condemnations of the 1910 report of the legislative investigating committee was the untreated disease and sickness found throughout the camps, much of which could be attributed to sick and healthy convicts sharing bath water and sleeping quarters.

J.S. Calvin, writing of his own experiences at the Farris Farm in 1898, stated, "And the prisoners were all turned in there together and the bunks were all in the center of the building like a Baptist pallet. The sick and well all staid [sic] in there together, and as most of the men that went out there with me were new men, right from jail, it was only a few days until more than half of them were down with the fever myself among the number."4

Three years earlier, in 1895, John Shotwell wrote of the conditions at the wood camp near Alto, Texas, "I slept in an old straw bunk four years, and it was never aired or sunned, and during all that time I never had a bath."5

Mills, who did considerable traveling around at various camps, described the mattresses at the Burleson and John Farm in 1910: "Our sleeping place was two rows of wooden frame bunks extending from one end of the room to the other with a small aisle between them. The bunks were built three deep. The beds were made of corn shucks, and it was nothing unusual to find a whole ear of corn in one of the mattresses...."

He also describes the day that conditions "improved" at the farm: "In 1916 one day we boys came in from work to find our shuck mattresses replaced with soft hay mattresses. This was the first improvement that I remember. Of course, later came the good cotton mattresses they are using today."6

But in many ways these inmates being assigned bunks, no matter how unsanitary or uncomfortable, were still far better off than some of the other convicts being leased out.

In the 1910 *Report of the Penitentiary Investigating Committee* one of the members, C.B. Hudspeth, wrote a dissenting opinion in which he outlined some of the inhumane living quarters he had witnessed as a committee member and recalled that such conditions had existed, with tacit prison administrator's approval, for several years including:

Twenty-six years ago [1884] a legislative committee saw forty convicts housed in one board room on the Wynne farm, some of them sick with pneumonia, and without one stove in the coldest weather ever felt in Texas until then.

At that time, in mid-summer, men were confined in box cars at night, and some pulled out dead next morning from that Calcutta death box.

A State Senator [Mr. Gibbs of Dallas] described the method of housing convicts while working on railroads; a few gum logs across a railroad ditch, under which the men entered by a hole, and over which the sergeant watched, gun in hand, until next morning, as one would watch a den of snakes.[7]

From the bug-infested mattresses of Huntsville to the "Calcutta death boxes" on the tracks of the Texas State Railroad, it appears that working a sixteen-hour day in the hot Texas sun didn't guarantee a good night's sleep.

---

1   Favor, Charles A., *Twenty-Two Months in the Texas Penitentiary*, pg. 29.
2   Wilkinson, J.L., *The Trans-Cedar lynching and the Texas Penitentiary*, pp. 133-4.
3   Mills, Bill, *25 Years Behind Prison Bars*, pg. 25.
4   Calvin, J.S., *Buried alive, or, A term in the Texas State Prison, 1898-1902: a chapter from real life*, pg. 38.
5   Shotwell, John, *A Victim of Revenge or Fourteen Years in Hell*, pg. 11.
6   Mills, pg. 9.
7   *Report of the Penitentiary Investigating Committee including All Exhibits and Testimony Taken by the Committee*, pg. 23.

Chapter Eleven

1874

Schribner's Monthly Report to the World

Texas Prison Interview with Kiowa Chief Satanta

The convict labor is contracted for, and is of great value in the building of the railways and the clearing of forests. As a rule, the men are worked from dawn to dark, and then conveyed to some near point, to be locked up in cars or barracks constructed especially for them. They are constantly watched, working or sleeping; and the records of the Penitentiary show many a name against which is written, "Killed while trying to escape."

We frequently passed large gangs of the convicts chopping logs in the forest by the roadside; they were ranged in regular rows, and their axes rose and fell in unison. When they had finished one piece of work, the stern voice of the supervisor called them to another, and they moved silently and sullenly to the indicated task.

In 1872 *Scribner's Monthly* assigned two young reporters the task of traveling throughout the American South with the instructions to "take the time you need, travel the miles that need to be covered. Come back and prepare for us a definitive account of what Reconstruction has meant to the Old South."

The two reporters, Edward King, a journalist, and James Wells Champney, a talented illustrator—both in their twenties—spent over a year doing just that: interviewing, traveling, investigating, recording, exploring, and documenting.

The result was a massive 800-page book published in Glasgow, Scotland, in 1875. One section of this unique journal involved their travels through Texas in 1874, and one century later that section was reprinted under the title *Texas: 1874*.[1] In it, King and Champney give us a unique look at Texas and Texans in the decade after the Civil War.

One chapter, titled "Pictures from Prison and Field," includes a train trip from Houston to Huntsville and a visit to the state penitentiary there. The authors describe the encountering of a "convict train" and leased convict laborers working alongside the railroad tracks. Using the vernacular of their period, they refer to Negroes as "Sambo and Cuffee" and describe them in generally derogatory terms while, at the same time, acknowledging the near return to prewar slavery by sentencing them to the state prison system.

Texas: 1874 is unusual in that it gives a view of the convict lease system from the perspective of outsiders, men not convicted of any crime and therefore not inclined to vent their anger and frustration at the institution.

"The sight of the 'convict train' is one of the experiences of Texan travel which still clings like a horrid nightmare in my memory," King wrote. He and Champney happened upon such a sight at some unnamed small Texas town just as the sun was setting, and King provides a pitiful image: "…the abject, cowering mass of black and white humanity in striped uniform had crouched down upon the platform cars; to see the alert watchmen standing at each end of every car with their hands upon their cocked and pointed rifles; to see the relaxed muscles and despairing faces of the overworked gang, was more than painful."

In 1874 J. Wells Champney sketched this Texas inmate work crew clearing woods beside a railroad track. Champney would later become a very successful artist so this rendition of the convict lease period may be one of the earliest illustrations of Texas inmates and is probably historically accurate. King, Edward, and J. Wells Champney, *Texas: 1874* (Houston: Cordovan Press, 1974), extracted from *The Great South* (Glasgow: Blackie and Son, 1875).

He describes, in a narrative directed toward a national reading audience, the convict labor system and the contracting of inmates for the building of railroads and other industrial work. He comments on their work schedules—dawn to dark—and their living conditions in boxcars or temporary buildings.

He also noted ominously that armed guards continuously supervise them and that the prison records indicate a considerable number of them are "killed while trying to escape."

At Huntsville, he found it unusual that inmates were routinely seen moving through the streets in chain gangs doing all kinds of manual labor for various businesses. Referring to the black inmates and their convictions for often "trivial offences," King writes: "Sambo and Cuffee have found the way of the transgressor unduly hard in Texas and most of the Southern States, since the war liberated them. Any unlucky blackamoor can be sentenced to a year on the 'convict train' for offenses as minor as not being able to explain how they got a ragged coat or twenty-five cent script."

"The main penitentiary unit in Huntsville," he writes, "is completely surrounded by armed guards. Inside, the shops are light and cheery, and the men and women, even the 'lifers,' who have stained their hands with blood, look as contented in the cotton spinning room as the ordinary factory hand does after a few years of eleven hours' toil daily. The prisoners make shoes, clothing, furniture and wagons, weave good cottons and woolens, and it is even proposed to set them at building cars."

Champney provides two excellent illustrations: one of a convict work crew on the roadside and another of an inmate inside the Huntsville unit. The Huntsville prisoner was alleged to be the infamous Kiowa chief Satanta.

Satanta and Big Tree, both high-ranking chiefs and warriors of the Kiowa, had been sentenced to prison for seven counts of murder for their part in the Warren wagontrain raid in 1871. Sentenced to hang, both men had their sentences commuted to life in prison and had entered Huntsville in 1871 but were paroled in 1873.

Both warriors, however, immediately participated in the Red River Wars of 1874 and had their paroles revoked and were rearrested. Satanta was returned to Huntsville on September 17, 1874, just as King and Champney were making their tour of Texas.

J. Wells Champney sketched Kiowa chief Satanta at the Huntsville prison in 1874. The sketch would be published in Glasgow the following year and distributed throughout Europe and the United States. Satanta would be dead within a few years—allegedly committing suicide inside the prison.

King, Edward, and J. Wells Champney, *Texas: 1874* (Houston: Cordovan Press, 1974), extracted from *The Great South* (Glasgow: Blackie and Son, 1875).

King recalled, "In a corridor of the Penitentiary I saw a tall, finely formed man, with bronzed complexion, and long, flowing, brown hair—a man princely in carriage, and on whom even the prison garb seemed elegant. It was Satanta, the chief of the Kiowas, who with his brother chief, Big Tree, is held to account for murder."

With the help of another inmate, whom King refers to as "a venerable bigamist," he was able to converse briefly in Spanish to the infamous Native American leader.

"Satanta had stepped into the work-room, where he was popularly supposed to labor, although he never performed a stroke of work, and had seated himself on a pile of oakum," King records. Oakum was a mixture of hemp or jute fiber treated with tar and used as caulking. While Satanta was seated, Champney drew the inmate in a striped suit sitting in shavings against a wooden barrel.

Big Tree was also present: "...briskly at work in another apartment plaiting a chair seat, and vigorously chewing tobacco. His face was clear cut and handsome, his coal black hair swept his shoulders, and he paused only to brush it back, give us a swift glance, and then turn briskly to his plaiting as before."

At this point, King may have mistaken the identity of the other Native American. In the fall of 1874, Big Tree was imprisoned at Fort Sill, in Oklahoma, until the Kiowas were finally defeated in December 1874.

King does not give any details of his interpreted "interview" with Satanta other than to observe afterwards that "The course pursued toward these Indians seems the proper one; it is only by imposing upon them the penalties to which other residents of the State are subject that they can be taught their obligations."

While *Texas: 1874* creates a very negative image of the convicts working on the railroad and highway work squads,

King is favorably impressed with the administration of the main prison unit itself, claiming that it is being leased from the State by enterprising persons who make it "a real industrial school albeit a severe one." He concludes his narrative by commenting on the favorable conditions at Huntsville as compared to most of the Texas county jails.

Chief Satanta would serve four years at Huntsville after the "interview" with Edward King, and on October 11, 1878, it was alleged he slashed his wrists. As he was being escorted to the second floor of the prison hospital, he jumped off the landing and killed himself. His death was shrouded by controversy, however, and even today there are critics who believe he was the victim of a staged suicide, and in reality yet another murder victim of prison officials.

---

1   King, Edward and J. Wells Champney, *Texas: 1874* (Houston: Cordovan Press, 1974), extracted from *The Great South* (Glasgow: Blackie and Son, 1875).

Chapter Twelve

The Uncle with the Neck Chains

Bud Russell was born in 1875, the period in which the earliest of these prison narratives were written. In 1905 he was the constable in Hill County, transferring convicted prisoners to the Burleson and John Farm. In 1908 he became the assistant transfer agent for the prison system working under John Luther.[1]

When Luther became the warden of the Huntsville unit in 1914, Bud Russell became the chief (and only) transfer agent for the prison system. It was a job he would hold until his retirement in 1944.

Prior to 1922 he crisscrossed the state of Texas by train, picking up convicted criminals from county courthouses, shackling them by neck chains, and transporting them under armed guard to the Texas prison system. In 1922 he began using an oversized flatbed truck with a frame of boilerplate and heavy wire mesh cage.

Although he traveled widely to pick up his charges, Bud Russell and his truck always ended up at Huntsville, therefore his vehicle became known as the "One-Way Wagon." Huntsville is still the only community in Texas offering bus service to all 254 counties.

From 1922 until his retirement in 1944, it's estimated he drove over 3.9 million miles collecting inmates from Texas counties, forty-five states, and even convicts from Mexico and Canada. Of the 115,000 inmates he transported, only one ever escaped, and that was because Russell chose not to kill him.

For a man with such a background, it would be expected that he would also be the most hated man in Texas. But just the opposite was the case. Almost without exception, inmates and former convicts recalled his transporting and treatment of them with respect.

In his miles around the state, he picked up and transported, at one time or another, almost every desperate criminal the Texas law officers could arrest and the courts could convict. His wards included such gangsters as Clyde and Buck Barrow, Raymond Hamilton, Joe Palmer, Charlie Frazier, and Clyde Thompson. His reputation among prisoners was so established that the infamous Joe Palmer and Raymond Hamilton requested he witness their highly publicized executions in 1935. Almost from the beginning of his career, he became known among inmates simply as "Uncle Bud."

Bud Russell, Chief Transfer Agent, Texas Prison System (Circa: 1920).
Photo courtesy of Robert H. Russell

But most of Bud Russell's exploits took place from 1908 through 1944, in many cases years after the narratives of the men who had worked the lease system.

However one narrative gives us a rare account of Bud Russell in the early days of his transporting convicts by train, at a period when he was the assistant transfer agent. Bill Mills, who would eventually serve seven prison sentences in state and federal prisons, started his convict career in 1910 out of Hunt County, Texas.

There, on December 4, he and thirteen other inmates were lined up in pairs and chained together by the necks with a long chain running along each line of prisoners. Then came the announcement, "Boys, get ready, Uncle Bud is here!"

Despite the fact he felt the inmates were "yoked like oxen," Mills also recalled, "…I want to state that Mr. Russell is one of the finest men whom I have ever met and any prisoner will tell you that he will threat you right if you will let him."[2]

In 1910, according to Mills, the prison system assigned inmates to the nearest prison from where they were convicted, and he was escorted by train and Bud Russell to the Burleson and John Farm near Blum, Texas. There, he was loaded onto a horse-drawn wagon and placed under the custody of armed prison guards.

Bud Russell had completed another successful transfer of his prisoners, just fourteen of the estimated 115,000 convicts he would successfully transfer over the course of his career.

Bud Russell's transition from train to "One-Way Wagon" in 1922 was a gradual transition, because in 1923 Milt Good recalled that he was on a chain with other convicted criminals that were escorted on a train by Bud Russell from Dallas to Corsicana. At times, when he had a large number of convicts, Russell would resort to train travel after 1922.

Like Mills, Good comments on Russell's demeanor with inmates: "Bud Russell was a sincere friend of the unfortunate men in prison, and don't forget for a minute that they know their friends. He is kind to all, and even the worst ones like him and respect him for his good sense and sympathy." [3]

Good would eventually escape from Huntsville and spend several months at liberty before being recaptured in Antlers, Oklahoma, and extradited back to Fort Worth. There, he reports, Bud Russell and the One-Way Wagon "came and took me back to Huntsville."[4]

Almost to a man, these narratives spanning 1875 to 1925 relate the humiliation and hatred these convicted men felt toward the neck chains they were forced to wear as they were transferred from county jail to state prison.

Given that universal hatred for their situation, it is amazing that the man who was responsible for guarding and transporting them would enjoy such a favorable reputation among the men he was escorting to what many referred to as "hell in Texas." Most amazing is that they would refer to him as "Uncle Bud."

---

1   Although Bud Russell is not well known in contemporary Texas correctional institutions, he had achieved a near-legendary reputation in the years leading up to World War II. Even today, inmates and guards refer to prison transfer busses as "chain busses" not knowing that it was Bud Russell who established the term and set the standards for transferring convicts throughout the state. His great-grandson, Robert H. Russell Jr., has provided the author with a wealth of information about his relative including these facts during an interview 08/15/01.

2   Mills, Bill, *25 Years Behind Prison Bars*, pp. 4-5.

3   Good, Milt, *Twelve Years in a Texas Prison*, pg. 22.

4   Ibid., pg. 36.

Chapter Thirteen

Run Like Hell, You Pitiful Soul

If conditions in the labor camps and plantation fields were as brutal as the narratives indicate, why didn't more of these leased convicts run for freedom? The answer is that they did—often in droves. For some, serving long terms or life sentences, the thought of forever enduring the pain, misery, starvation, whippings, and abuse in the camps was unbearable. For others, no doubt, the prospect of being shot in the back was preferable to continuing as they were living.

We know from the narratives and from state documents of the convict lease period that self-mutilation was rampant, ranging from cutting off body limbs to injecting kerosene under the skin to create terrible body rashes. Some even blinded themselves.

But others simply chose to risk death trying to escape. From the earliest records of the Texas prison system, the notation "killed while trying to escape" is found repeatedly.

The narratives of men who served time during the convict lease period, at least those who worked in the camps rather than the main units, are filled with escape accounts and the charges that guards routinely justified killing inmates by reporting the convict was attempting to escape, whether an actual escape was in progress or not.

Prison guards at Camp 2 of the Eastham Prison Farm (Circa: 1914). Note the prisoners peering through the celled window in the background.
Photo courtesy of Robert H. Russell and the Texas Prison Museum, Huntsville, Texas.

The pamphlet *It's Hell in a Texas Pen, the barbarous conditions as told by ex-convicts and unearthed by the Legislature* is filled with reports of guards using the excuse of "thwarting an escape" to kill inmates. One report claims that after an inmate was killed, the subsequent prison investigation suggested the convict was going to kill a dog so the guard was "protecting state property."

But both unsubstantiated and official reports indicate that leased convicts did attempt to escape, and the attempts were made often and were usually unsuccessful.

John Shotwell, writing of the late 1890s, recalled that "the desire to escape never dies" among leased convicts. "They feel that 10 years of that life is too terrible to bear with dogged patience and there is ever the thought that the continued hard life may bring them to the grave before sentence is ended."[1]

Henry Tomlin, the man who claimed to have suffered eighteen years of physical abuse as the result of refusing to work for prison officials, was particularly bitter of the state policy of offering a standard twenty-five-dollar reward for escaped convicts during that period. "...every squatter or nester in hearing shoulders a shotgun and turns himself a man hunter in the hope of getting the paltry reward. I say every one, when I only mean a certain low class of fellows do this; not for the purpose of serving the State and upholding the law, but just for the money than may be in it."[2]

Tomlin also describes the methods used to apprehend prison escapees in the 1800s: "All the spare guards are run out with dogs and guns and a merciless hunt is at once organized and is kept up until the poor unfortunate is again captured or lost entirely; and instances of the latter are few indeed, as the telegraph and telephone and railroads are brought into requisition, and such a thing as a man getting away is indeed a rarity."[3]

But the stories of the attempts themselves are the most interesting, whether the inmate failed or succeeded. Given the inhuman work conditions of the lease camps, most escapes were simply crude dashes for freedom with little forethought or planning.

John Dunn, however, did carefully plan and set up his successful escape from a lease camp on the Sabine River in the 1880s. During flooding, Dunn was laboring on a work crew trying to build a levy when he made his break. It was a planned break and he was just waiting for the right moment. His ankle chains had been previously filed through so he could snap them off by hand. He had followed the cardinal rule of keeping his plan to himself, but when he made his break, two other convicts attempted to follow him in their chains, and he assumes the subsequent gunfire killed them.

This 1905 state prison reward notice offers $25 for the apprehension of a Tom Nalley who had escaped from the Robertson Farm in Ft. Bend County. The notice and reward amount were standard for the period. Nalley was convicted of horse and mule theft out of Anderson County.
Author's collection.

He ran to the riverbank, got stuck in the mud, and then dived into the swollen river with bullets hitting the water all around him. In the rushing floodwaters, he was struck by a large log and desperately hung on to it. He almost drowned but managed to ride it downriver to safety and an eventual successful escape. He headed to Mexico and eventually relocated in New Mexico and lived into his nineties without ever returning to Texas prisons.[4]

John Shotwell, whose angry and bitter narrative of his prison time in Texas covers the period 1895 to 1909, escaped the infamous Calvert Coal Mines by jumping into the river and swimming away as the guards shot into the water. He successfully escaped by following a rail line and then spending twenty days hiding in the woods while stealing food, clothing, and a gun from nearby farmhouses. He would eventually leave Texas and travel throughout the U.S. and into Mexico before returning to Jefferson, Texas, where he was recaptured.[5]

In 1910 Bill Mills began the first of five prison terms in Texas. It would only be in 1938, after twenty-five years in prison cells, that he would leave prison for the final time. During that stretch, which included federal prison time, he recalled many escapes.

One involved Dock Newton (Mills spelled his name "Doc").[6] After escaping prison in Texas, Newton and his brothers would eventually travel north and Dock would be critically wounded in a sensational 1924 Illinois train robbery that would result in federal prison time.

But while Mills' account includes mention of Dock Newton, Mills himself had been dead for many years when Newton made his last robbery attempt in Rowena, Texas, in 1968. At age seventy-seven and some forty-four years after he had received his sentence for the now legendary Illinois train robbery, Newton was captured and sentenced to prison again.

After eight months in a prison hospital, he was released and died in a nursing home in 1974 at age eighty-three.

Bill Mills, it appears, was not the only Texas inmate in early 1900s to struggle with overcoming the criminal habit.

Mills also recalls the escape of the notorious Tom Slaughter from the Rusk unit in which he kidnapped prison officials, had cooks prepare and serve a meal to him and the captives, and then escaped the unit.[7]

During the 1920s Beecher Deason observed several escape attempts and participated in a few himself. His first attempt involved riding away from a work crew on a mule then swimming the Trinity River. He recalled, "It certainly gave me a curious feeling to slip around and keep under cover like some wild beast. Every human instinct in me revolted against it."[8] He was quickly caught.

During the cold November months of 1925, he escaped the Blueridge Farm by removing part of the building roof, swimming a drainage ditch, and later floating several miles down a creek while holding a wooden pole. Workers on an oilrig eventually turned him in.[9]

In 1928 Deason and several other inmates were "herding birds" (acting as human scarecrows to keep birds off the corn crop) on the Clemens Farm in Brazoria County, when he made another attempt. This time he ran through the corn field into woods and made a zigzag course, climbed up and down several trees to throw off the dogs, and ran in circles and backtracked. He eluded the hounds and eventually found a rural house, but he was so exhausted he asked the farmer to call the prison authorities.[10]

So escape attempts from the convict lease camps were common. Most were crude attempts almost always ending in recapture, John Dunn being the notable exception. But many, many attempts ended in death.

Shotwell, writing of the crude inmate burial ground outside the infamous Alto wood camp, recalled that those who were buried at the Lone Pine Graveyard had died from other than natural causes. Many committed suicide and still more were killed in attempting escape.

1   Shotwell, John, *A Victim of Revenge or Fourteen Years in Hell*, pg. 26.
2   Tomlin, Henry, *Henry Tomlin, the man who fought the brutality and oppression of the ring in the state of Texas for eighteen years and won*, pp. 26-27.
3   Ibid., pg. 27.
4   Evans, Max, *Long John Dunn of Taos, From Texas Outlaw to New Mexico Hero*, pg. 49.
5   Shotwell, pp. 22-25.
6   Mills, Bill, *25 Years Behind Prison Bars*, pg. 36.
7   Ibid., pp. 36-37.
8   Deason, Beecher, *Seven Years in Texas Prisons*, pg. 14.
9   Ibid., pp. 20-21.
10 Ibid., pp. 17-18.

(1880s)

Long John Dunn of Taos

The Texas Prison Memoir of John Dunn

This was my moment. I strained against the chain, and it snapped. It was now or never. I raced down the river, hoping to reach the seclusion of the thick brush that abounded there. Two other prisoners, sensing that something was going to happen, had been watching me. They followed, but were slowed by their chains. I heard shots and screams. I figured the guards must have killed the other two.

The sheer brutality and oppressiveness of the convict lease period guaranteed some inmates would try to escape captivity but also insured that almost none would ever succeed. Of the narratives written during this period, those few who did successfully escape from the lease camps or prison farms would always somehow be recaptured and returned to the system—often with terrible retaliatory consequences by the guards.

One rare successful escape did occur on a convict lease camp near the Sabine River in the 1880s. While the escape in itself was unusual, what really made this particular effort so unique was the fact that the inmate was wearing a ball and chain at the time. Most unusual, however, was the fact that the escapee was never caught or returned to prison and lived to write his account of the experience.

In 1947 a local writer in the Taos, New Mexico, area received an inquiry from a well-known ninety-year-old local man. Although the old-timer had a suspect reputation and personal history, he was also held in high regard, well liked, and generally respected as a local character. Realizing that his life was nearly over, the old man claimed, he wanted a writer to record his life experiences and "put a few rumors to rest." One of those "rumors" involved the allegation that he was an escaped convict from Texas—still wanted by the Texas Rangers.

An agreement was reached, and the elderly man began dictating his life history to his selected biographer. Recalling his eight decades of life and experiences, the old man began by describing his childhood in Texas. He recalled the hungry and fearful years of the Civil War followed by the later difficulties during Reconstruction.

As the biographer collected notes, the old man also talked of his days plowing behind a mule on a Texas cotton farm, working as a cowboy on the early trail drives, and his apprenticeship in the dusty saloons where he learned to cheat gamblers out of their hard-earned money.

But along with these experiences came involvement in criminal behavior including cattle stealing—a hanging offense in Texas at that time. After killing a man, he fled and traveled widely before settling in New Mexico.

There, safely out of the jurisdiction of the Texas Rangers, he spent the next several decades at various endeavors while becoming wealthy and prosperous and developing a well-recognized reputation locally.

He died in 1953, but at the time of his storytelling in Taos in 1947, he had already been promoting himself as the man transformed "from Texas outlaw to New Mexico hero" for many years.

His final biography, obviously dictated in his favorable terms, is almost completely devoid of verifiable dates, places, and names—the storyteller admitting ambiguity to protect parts of his past and certain people he had known.

But somewhere in the middle of his life story, between Texas and New Mexico, there were two episodes about which he was particularly ambiguous—his murder conviction and his time incarcerated in the Texas prison system.

The storyteller was John Dunn, and his biography was published in 1959 titled *Long John Dunn of Taos, From Texas Outlaw to New Mexico Hero*, as written by Max Evans. And while it gives little factual information, it does provide colorful musings and observations of a wild period in Texas history, including a short period on a chain gang.

John Dunn was born in Victoria, Texas, in 1857 into a poor farming family. After a failed attempt to resettle in Missouri, his father returned the family to Texas and attempted farming in the Waco area.

Dunn later recalled the Civil War years when his father was away serving in the Confederacy while the family lived in constant fear of Indian raids around the Waco area. Then came the Reconstruction period when his wounded father returned home unable to work and the family struggled to survive. A turning point in his life, he recalled, was the time he had to dig his own father's grave because the family was too poor to hire an undertaker.

To earn money, he hired out plowing cotton fields but quickly became involved in petty criminal activity, something that escalated into the felony act of stealing a horse. To evade the law, he traveled to the Abilene area and worked as a cowboy on the early cattle drives. But the outlaw lifestyle had taken hold, and he soon became involved in cattle theft and gambling activities.

Back in Texas, he discovered his older sister had married an alcoholic who physically abused her. A confrontation escalated into a fistfight in which Dunn killed his brother-in-law. After his arrest for murder he was tried, found guilty, and sentenced to life in the state penitentiary. He was then transferred from county jail to Rusk prison.

He provides no dates, but the period of the cattle-drive era and the completion of the Rusk penitentiary in 1883 suggest it was in the late 1880s, which would have meant Dunn was in his thirties.

Dunn never denied striking the blow that killed his brother-in-law; in fact, he later bragged, "It was my first killing." He claims his murder conviction was the result of "no money, few friends, and although the dead man was a no-good sot, he had relatives in influential positions."[1]

After the jury found him guilty of murder and the judge sentenced him to life in prison, he was transferred with two other prisoners to the state penitentiary at Rusk. After processing into the prison, he remained at Rusk for three weeks until he was assigned to a work crew and transferred to a farm somewhere on the Sabine River. Again, Dunn provides no dates or a name of the prison farm, but his narrative leaves no doubt it was one of the infamous lease farms typical in Texas during that period.

He was assigned to what could only be called a Texas chain gang. "Prisoners had long chains locked on their legs, which made a big raw sore before they could get used to dragging the chain. We couldn't pick these chains up to walk, except by special permission from the guards."[2]

He discovered that certain inmates were having contraband files brought into the camp and arranged to get one.

Then at night when he had an element of privacy, he would work on filing through the chain. Leaving enough metal to hold the chain together until he could break it by hand at the right time, he continued working in the camp during the days with the ball and chain attached to his ankle.

Then one day—and again he provides no dates—the camp was inundated by heavy rains that caused the nearby Sabine River to flood. His work crew was dispatched to build a dirt levee to stem the flooding, and Dunn saw his chance for escape.

"I asked a guard if it was all right to pick up the chain. The answer was yes, and all the prisoners were granted permission to do this," he recalled many decades later.[3] This was his moment and he picked up the chain, snapped it open, and bolted for the river.

Claiming two other prisoners also attempted to join him but were unable to run with their chains, he recalled hearing shots and screams but didn't know if the convicts had been shot and killed.

Without the chain, he was able to run but almost immediately became mired in the mud gumbo on the riverbank, so he dived into the swollen and raging floodwaters and managed to grab a large floating log.

Dragging himself from the water on the opposite riverbank, he walked to a nearby farmhouse and raided the pantry for three large cans of black pepper, which he used in an attempt to throw the inevitable bloodhounds off his trail.

The second day, he claims, he killed a rabbit with a rock and ate part of it raw. Then he spent several days traveling south along railroad tracks before stealing a rifle at another farmhouse.

He then worked his way farther south into Mexico and began a lifetime of flight from the Texas Rangers. His short time in the prison work camp had left a profound impression upon him: He referred several times in his biography to his recurring fear of having that chain reattached to his ankle.

Once, he claimed, during those fugitive years he was caught near Mobeetie, Texas, only to escape the courtroom before sentencing. On that occasion he managed to get out of Texas only by hiding in a wagon beneath a load of hay being hauled into New Mexico.

New Mexico would become his permanent home, and he would live around the Taos and Red River areas, continuing his criminal and illegal activities, until his death in 1953—bragging that the state of Texas had given him forty years (life?) in the state penitentiary and that he had "given them back thirty-nine years three months and some few days."[4]

He died May 22, 1953, a well-known and colorful character in his adopted New Mexico. Before his death, he claimed the account over his murder conviction and escape from prison was closed on the books for good when Texas issued him a "full and free" pardon. As was the case throughout his biography, however, he neglected to offer dates, names, or any facts to back up his claim.

Like much of John Dunn's life, his account of his time in the Texas prison system is undocumented and almost certainly overstated. *Long John Dunn of Taos, From Texas Outlaw to New Mexico Hero* makes clear, however, that the time he actually did serve on that chain gang in Texas instilled a fear of ankle chains that remained with him the remainder of his long life.

1   Evans, Max, *Long John Dunn of Taos, From Texas Outlaw to New Mexico Hero* (Santa Fe, NM: Clear Light Publishers, 1959), pg. 48.

2   Ibid.

3   Ibid., pg. 49.

4   Ibid., pg. 143.

Chapter Fifteen

The Progressive Reporter from San Antonio

The first two decades of the 1900s is often referred to as the Progressive Era—both in national and in state political histories. Social issues such as industrialization and the related worker issues, tenement farming, universal education, and children's rights began to be examined by newspapers, schools, and government. One of the issues at the center of controversy during the Progressive Era was that of prison reform.

As the twentieth century began, Texas prisons were deeply entrenched in the philosophy of the convict lease system despite a growing number of critics and an increasing preponderance of evidence that Texas inmates were being grossly abused.

Most Texans, however, were preoccupied with the issues of better roads and schools, mechanizing the agricultural sector, and urban development, therefore the voices of those condemning the convict lease system were for the most part ignored or unheard.

It wasn't until a frustrated Reverend Jake Hodges of the Huntsville prison unit approached a young cub reporter that the convict lease system became a prominent social issue in Texas.

In the fall of 1908, a young reporter for the *San Antonio Express* named George Waverly Briggs began a series of investigative articles on the realities of the convict lease system and the Texas prison system in general.

Writing in a series of Sunday edition issues from December 6, 1908, through January 10, 1909, Briggs disclosed allegations of inmate abuse and torture as well as corruption and financial mismanagement among prison officials.

On December 6, 1908, the *San Antonio Express* ran a front-page headline titled "Penal System of Texas is a Failure," in which Briggs proclaimed "Under Present System, Reformation of Prisoners Is Practically Impossible and Penal Institutions Are the Prey of Political Spoiling."[1]

The following week he investigated the conditions of women prisoners in the prison system and disclosed, among other facts, that sixty-seven female prisoners were being kept on the Eastham farm without any female supervision and that long-term female prisoners were giving birth while incarcerated.[2] His allegation that a female prisoner was forced to work in the cotton fields during her pregnancy and actually gave birth in one of the dirt rows in the field only to be forced back out to the field in the afternoon after lunch was especially damning after publication.

His December 20, 1908 column advocated, ironically, that Texas convicts be assigned to road gangs.[3] In reality, much of his argument was that Texas prisoners be removed from private leases and placed under direct state supervision and worked in the open where the public could monitor their conditions.

The December 27, 1908 issue investigated the health conditions of the prisons and work camps with the conclusion that health and sanitation were sacrificed or completely ignored by the private leasers in attempts to increase their profits even more.[4]

On January 3, 1909, his investigation turned to the treatment of inmates by the prison guards with the conclusions that gross maltreatment of inmates and ignoring of the rules of punishment were rampant among underpaid guards and that prison administrative officials were content to allow it and even cover up inmate allegations to protect the guards.[5]

The sixth and final report on January 10 again recommended that Texas prisoners be put to work building much-needed roads and that the policy of leasing out the prisoners to profit-hungry corporations be halted.[6]

The impact of Briggs' series was immediate and widespread. Texans, as individuals and in groups, began to petition the legislature for reformation of the convict lease system. Religious groups joined the demand for an official government investigation, and the governor finally, but reluctantly, agreed and named a legislative committee to do the investigation and report.

The result of that assignment was the *Report of the Penitentiary Investigating Committee including All Exhibits and Testimony Taken by the Committee*, published by the Texas House of Representatives in August 1910, which, legally at least, led to the abandonment of the convict lease system in Texas.

As for Briggs, he left the staff of the *Express* in 1910 and became managing editor of the *Austin Statesman* briefly, reported for the *Dallas Morning News*, and edited the *Galveston News*. His reports concerning the convict lease system would be published as a book titled *The Texas Penitentiary*

The 1910 legislative report on the prison camps and farm units specifically listed sanitation as a major concern. Inmates were using gallon pails as commodes in their cells. This photograph suggests the condition had only marginally improved immediately after the convict lease years.
Photo source: Texas State Archives

This photograph, probably taken in the 1930s, indicates Texas inmates lived in squalor and filth. Amazingly, the prisoners during the convict lease system would probably have considered this a vast improvement over their conditions in the work camps. Photo source: Texas State Archives, courtesy of Jester III unit, Texas Department of Criminal Justice.

As antiquated, unsafe, and unsanitary as this prison industry shop appears, convicts during the lease system would cut off fingers and toes to get off the work farms and be assigned to a job in one of these shops. Photo source: Texas State Archives, courtesy of Jester III unit, Texas Department of Criminal Justice.

in 1910 and would result in his appointment as a commissioner of the prison system.

He would eventually become involved in finance and banking and would serve as commissioner of insurance and banking as well as vice-president of several major banks in Texas. He wrote the *Digest of Texas Insurance and Banking Laws* and was involved in the drafting and passing of several legislative laws concerning banking matters.

At the time of his death in 1957, he was director of the *Dallas Morning News* and involved in many civic organizations.

1   "Penal System of Texas is a Failure," *San Antonio Express*, December 6, 1908.

2   "Treatment of These Women is Inhuman," *San Antonio Express*, December 13, 1908.

3   "Roads are Best Places for Prisoners," *San Antonio Express*, December 20, 1908.

4   "Profit Making Precludes Proper Care," *San Antonio Express*, December 27, 1908.

5   "Atrocities by the Guards Go Unpunished," *San Antonio Express*, January 3, 1909.

6   "Roads Can Be Built By Prisoners," *San Antonio Express*, January 10, 1909.

Chapter Sixteen

(1900-1910)

The Trans-Cedar Lynching and the Texas Penitentiary

The Texas Prison Memoir of J.L. Wilkinson

I have known men to inflict personal injury upon themselves in order to get off of the farms. I knew two who cut their heel strings [tendon of Achilles], and ruined themselves for life in order to exchange the perpetual torment on the farm for the lesser one within the walls.

...the next morning, as we all came out from breakfast, a boy about eighteen years of age dodged out from the line, ran to the wood pile and chopped his hand off at the wrist. This sent him to the hospital. The Superintendent went up, and on asking why he cut his hand off, received the reply, that he did it to keep from going back to the farm; and added that had he not known that his widowed mother would have grieved for him, he would have cut his throat, rather than go back.

On August 22, 1900, eight recently convicted prisoners arrived by wagon at the gates of Rusk penitentiary for processing into the state prison system. The eight men were from

Henderson County, where they had been convicted of murder involving a horrendous lynching near Athens, Texas.

One of those eight men that day included J.L. Wilkinson, sentenced to life in prison, and as was so often the case with incoming prisoners, continuing to proclaim his innocence of the charges.

J.L. Wilkinson was convicted of participating in a lynching in Henderson County, Texas, and sentenced to prison in 1900. He served a decade at Rusk, and after release, published his account of the trial and his imprisonment. His account in many ways reflects the account of Henry Tomlin. Wilkinson, J.L., *The Trans-Cedar lynching and the Texas Penitentiary; being a plain account of the lynching and the circumstances leading up to it, also a presentation of conditions as they exist in our state penitentiaries*, (Dallas: Johnston Printing and Advertising Co., No date given).

This inmate, like Henry Tomlin before him, made it his personal mission to take on the state of Texas and its prison officials. By his own suggestion, "old Joe Wilkinson was the bull-headiest old devil sent to that prison." He also stated later, "I went into the penitentiary fully determined to look after old Joe regardless of the conditions into which he had been driven."

By the time he left prison a decade later, there were probably more than a few guards and prison officials who would have agreed.

Sometime after leaving Rusk, no date is given, Wilkinson published his memoir titled *The Trans-Cedar lynching and the*

Texas Penitentiary; being a plain account of the lynching and the circumstances leading up to it, also a presentation of conditions as they exist in our state penitentiaries.

The title alone suggests the intent of Wilkinson's booklet— to present his case to the public with regards to the conditions inside Texas prisons.

The trial and conviction of Wilkinson and his co-defendants had attracted newspaper attention throughout Texas and in some of the larger circulation newspapers outside the state. The crime had involved the lynching of three well-known Henderson County men; and the trial had been conducted under the suspicion that the sheriff was conspiring to gain convictions at any cost.

The murders had aroused emotions on the part of several families involved—relatives of both defendants and victims. At one point the emotions surrounding the case had become so intense the governor had ordered a company of Texas Rangers to the county to keep peace. A month-long court of inquiry was conducted, and sixteen men were arrested for the crime.

Several of the men turned state witnesses and testified against the others and in return for their testimony, were acquitted. The eight defendants they testified against were found guilty of murder and sentenced to life in prison.

One of those found guilty in that Henderson County courtroom was J.L. Wilkinson. He entered prison an extremely angry and bitter man, and *The Trans-Cedar lynching and the Texas Penitentiary* suggests he never got over that anger.

Wilkinson's first encounter at Rusk was a reception by the infamous Captain Ezell, whom Henry Tomlin had written about in *Henry Tomlin, the man who fought the brutality and oppression of the ring in the state of Texas for eighteen years and won.* Like Tomlin, Wilkinson immediately came into conflict with Ezell, "whose every word, action and visage stamped him a cruel brute in everything but form; and thus I judged him."

During processing, Wilkinson and the other new arrivals were photographed (the earliest narrative mention of cameras being used by the Bertillion officer), issued prison striped uniforms, and given shaves and haircuts. They were fed a hasty meal of corn bread, cow peas, and fat meat and within an hour of arrival at the prison were taken to the wood yard and ordered to start splitting wood.

Wilkinson's bullheadedness set in and he refused to pick up his axe and go to work, telling the guard, "I do not think a man of my age and disabilities is supposed to split wood; I did not do it at home, and I would not do it here."

He was not punished by the superintendent and, even more surprisingly, was given a job working on a crane with two one-armed men where there was little actual work to do. "I held this job for two years, working on the average of about two hours a day," he later wrote.

Wilkinson would find that his prison time at Rusk would not always be as accommodating, however, and like Henry Tomlin before him, he would discover that Captain Ezell would single him out for later retaliation as a consequence of his refusing to split wood.

The first alleged retaliation came in the form of Ezell taking Wilkinson's son and placing him in the dark cell on false charges. Wilkinson does not explain why his son was also in prison at Rusk (or if he was one of the eight other co-defendants), nor does he mention him after this incident in which he claims Ezell had his son removed from a good job in the prison hospital and locked in solitary confinement.

Claiming that Ezell was using punishment of his son to get back at him for his work refusal, Wilkinson swore that if the captain used the bat to beat his boy, "the whole State of Texas should know about it, for I would have had my inning regardless of consequences."

In this confrontation with Ezell, Wilkinson began undermining Ezell's authority by going directly to the prison superintendent, Colonel W.M. Lacy. It is at this time that he refers to himself as "old Joe Wilkinson…the bull-headiest old devil sent to that prison."

Like Henry Tomlin a few years earlier, J.L. Wilkinson vents pure hatred for the captain who was making his life miserable at Rusk:

> How Ezell ever got to be a part of the system is beyond my power to explain; if the looks of a man would keep him out; although many of his underlings, getting their cues from him, never hesitated to be as brutal as he, though they could never look it. Besides, his color should have been against him. He belonged to no yellow-haired, rosy-cheeked, blue-eyed race. He was not Indian, though his hair was black; it was inclined to curl. Of some mixed breed he evidently sprung, and both guards and inmates, noting his smutty complexion summed up their judgment in calling him "Smokey."

Ezell's sadistic character, Wilkinson claims, was such that he had killed twenty-six inmates by either beating them to death or working them until they dropped dead from sickness and exhaustion.

One specific murder he attributed to the brutal prison captain involved a teenaged boy by the name of Lightfoot, whom Wilkinson described as "delicate" in frame. This young inmate was very sickly and could not maintain the pace of work required in the fields. Although the camp doctor ordered the boy to the hospital, Ezell, or so Wilkinson claims, forced the young inmate out of the hospital bed and into the fields.

After two days Lightfoot was again returned to the hospital with a raging fever only to have Ezell again force him back into the field crew. That next day, Wilkinson alleges, the boy worked until evening before falling into uncontrollable chills. Then, before he could be returned to the prison unit and the penitentiary hospital, he went into convulsions and died in the field.

In an unsubstantiated "official report," Wilkinson alleges, Ezell and the other prison officials reported the death as the boy's own fault: "He had died as the result of eating so many raw potatoes they cramped him to death. Raw potatoes!"

Wilkinson also related another incident in which a sick inmate was worked to death in the field, and this incident is very similar to a report in the narrative *Henry Tomlin, the man who fought the brutality and oppression of the ring in the state of Texas for eighteen years and won.*

The inmate involved was identified simply as "Moseley," and the similarities of the narratives of Wilkinson and Tomlin suggest that there was either a factual basis for the allegation or that the two inmates later collaborated on their narratives.

In *The Trans-Cedar Lynching*, Wilkinson goes into some detail about the circumstances of this particular death in the field. Moseley had been leased out to one of the convict work farms in East Texas and had been returned to Rusk prison with five other inmates, in Wilkinson's words, "...as nearly driven, starved and beat to death as I ever saw men."

All of the men, except Moseley, allegedly died within two days. Moseley remained in the penitentiary hospital under the doctor's care for months before recovering enough to be assigned "light work" as a steward in the inmate mess hall.

As soon as he was released from his hospital bed, Wilkinson reports, Captain Ezell immediately had Moseley assigned to an outside work crew cutting wood.

Moseley, whom Wilkinson describes as still being emaciated and sickly, begged the captain not to send him out to the fields. His response was: "Go, or I will kick your guts out."

That first day the other convicts assumed Moseley's wood quota into their own work loads and allowed the sick inmate to stack the split wood, a relatively easy task. As a result, however, the already overworked inmates on the work crew were struggling to maintain their quotas to avoid a beating or assignment to the dark cell.

The second morning, Moseley again begged not to be sent to the field, and Ezell responded by telling the guards to "single him out and make him a full hand." Once in the field, the guards assigned Moseley a position on a crosscut saw, a job that required considerable strength and endurance.

Moseley attempted to do the work, but as a result of the effort in his condition, he collapsed over the handle of the saw and died. The guard's response, according to both Wilkinson and Tomlin, was to leave the body of the dead inmate lying over the saw throughout the day while the other crews worked around it. After the work squad had put in a full day's work, Moseley's body was loaded onto the wagon and carried back that evening.

Back at Rusk, Captain Ezell was informed of Moseley's death and responded, according to Wilkinson, by feigning surprise and shock. "There must be a mistake, as I regarded Moseley as one of the stoutest men in the prison," the officer allegedly stated. The official cause of death, according to both Tomlin and Wilkinson, was listed as "Died from 'natural' causes."

Like Tomlin's account, *The Trans-Cedar Lynching* offers no official documentation to verify this incident. Henry Tomlin's memoirs included a staged photograph of a convict whom he alleges was Moseley lying dead across a log and crosscut saw. Wilkinson simply offers more details to the allegation.

J.L. Wilkinson, in *The Trans-Cedar lynching and the Texas Penitentiary*, details an incident in which the feared Captain Ezell forced a sickly inmate named Moseley to work on the wood crews until the prisoner died. He was then left, according to Wilkinson, lying dead across the saw the rest of the day until the crew returned to the camp in the evening. Henry Tomlin also mentions the incident and offers this staged illustration.

Tomlin, Henry, *Henry Tomlin, the man who fought the brutality and oppression of the ring in the state of Texas for eighteen years and won. The story of how men traffic in the liberties and lives of their fellow men* (Dallas: Johnston Printing and Advertising Co., 1906).

At some unspecified date, a new prison superintendent was appointed at Rusk, and he brought in a new underkeeper named John Meeks. Meeks, Wilkinson claims, was "drunk the day he received his first month's pay, and never drew another sober breath during the four years he was in charge...."

One of the first changes in the new administration, especially under the control of Meeks, was to establish a wooden barrel of whiskey in the commissary—ostensibly for the use of the sick prisoners. But "the steward and others of the official family, like bees to water, went to that barrel so often that; together with what little was given the sick, a new barrel had to be brought in about once every two months," Wilkinson writes.

With key prison officials and selected inmates drunk much of the time, Wilkinson claims, the few services available to prisoners at Rusk quickly deteriorated. "It [the whiskey barrel] cost many a convict his life and helped to undermine the health of many others."

Inmates at Rusk from 1900 to 1910, according to Wilkinson, were afforded the "privilege" of purchasing outside necessities. Since the inmates were not paid for working, almost none had any money and the majority of the convict population was forced to live without decent food, underwear, socks, toothbrushes, and other toiletries necessary for personal health and sanitation.

Like virtually every other narrative of the convict lease period, Wilkinson describes in graphic detail the administering of the bat as a form of punishment. Ezell, not surprisingly, was credited with the most brutal beatings, and Wilkinson alleges the captain personally enjoyed the administration of the strapping and ignored the thirty-nine-lash limit to the point of giving "seventy-five or a hundred lashes."

Although he was never assigned outside the Rusk walls, Wilkinson was in a position to observe the dispatching and return of hundreds of unfortunate Texas prisoners who where shipped out to the "hellish" convict lease camps and the new state-owned prison farms in East Texas. From his position inside the Rusk walls, he reports seeing convicts returned from the work camps "scarred from head to heels from the use of the bat." It was from such a group of convicts that the young boy dodged out from the work line, ran to the wood pile, and chopped his hand off at the wrist rather than return to the camps.

The Trans-Cedar Lynching is one of the few narratives to mention the Reverend Jake Hodges, the Huntsville chaplain whose crusading efforts are credited by many for eventually bringing about the abolition of the convict lease system in Texas.

Wilkinson writes, "Jake Hodges either did not know that his business was merely to give dignity, and an outward show of morality to the system, or else he did not care so long as he saw his duty in a different light, and as soon as he got a correct sight on the situation he began to fire into and expose the inhumanity of the system as well as preach humility, long suffering and patience to the convicts."

Wilkinson probably had never met Hodges since the chaplain was assigned to the Huntsville unit and Wilkinson spent his entire decade in prison at Rusk. Rusk, however, also had a chaplain, unnamed in *The Trans-Cedar Lynching*, but Wilkinson recalls an incident involving the minister.

That Rusk chaplain had become despondent and dejected at his inability to convert the convicts at the penitentiary. Wilkinson claims to have asked the minister: "Do you think if it were possible for you to go to hell, and preach to the inmates there, they would be moved by what you would say?"

"No," the chaplain admitted, and Wilkinson then replied: "If there was ever a bunch of men in hell, this bunch is in it right now."

In this exchange, Wilkinson underscores what virtually every other inmate-written narrative of the convict lease period in Texas also advocated: As a prisoner in Texas from 1875 to 1925, a condemned man was sentenced to what amounted to "hell on earth."

Wilkinson concludes *The Trans-Cedar lynching and the Texas Penitentiary* with a list of grievances concerning the graft and mismanagement of the prison system in addition to the brutality. Wilkinson's narrative is similar to others of that period, namely those of Henry Tomlin and Charles Campbell, and yet his biased but clearly stated indictment makes excellent points:

> ...as I have repeatedly told you, the policy of the management of the system is to send only the most robust out upon the farms, and to bring back to the walls the mutilated and sick to be exchanged for well ones.
>
> Such a plan, if persisted in, would make a fountain of perpetual youth look like a swimming hole for cadavers.

Wilkinson, in *The Trans-Cedar Lynching*, presents a narrative very similar in many ways to *Henry Tomlin, the man who fought the brutality and oppression of the ring in the state of Texas for eighteen years and won*.

Henry Tomlin served time at Rusk from 1889 through 1904, at least four years during the period J.L. Wilkinson was also imprisoned there.

Another interesting fact is that both men published their prison memoirs with Johnston Printing and Advertising Company in Dallas—Tomlin in 1906 and Wilkinson's booklet not listing a date, but published sometime after his release in 1910.

Both men speak scathingly of the "Captain Ezell" at Rusk. And both narratives detail the death, allegedly because of Ezell, of the convict named Moseley, but there is no suggestion in either narrative that the two prisoners knew each other at Rusk or after their releases.

Like Tomlin's prison memoir, however, *The Trans-Cedar lynching and the Texas Penitentiary* gives a graphic description of prison life inside the foreboding walls of Rusk penitentiary a century ago.

And Wilkinson's description of the conditions at Rusk as "making a fountain of perpetual youth look like a swimming hole for cadavers" mirrors every other inmate narrative of the period.

Chapter Seventeen

The Infamous Calvert Coal Mines

Of the terrible stories to evolve from the sawmill camps, cotton plantations, and other work crews leased out during this period, probably the most infamous camp was one leased by the Houston and Texas Central Railway near Calvert, Texas, and operated as Southwestern Fuel and Manufacturing Company.

During the period of the convict lease system, the H&TC Railroad used leased convict labor to work the lignite mines in conditions so terrible the 1910 legislative investigating committee called for the immediate cancellation of the lease agreement with the railroad.

Of the various convict narratives during this period, only John Shotwell writes of having been assigned at Calvert. Not giving a specific date but writing of the period 1895 to 1909, he explains that he was assigned to the Calvert Coal Mines after having made several escape attempts. At the time he was sent there, he reports, there were fifty convicts leased out to the railroad.

"Of all the horrors that I had ever witnessed, there was none to compare with those coal mines," he later wrote. "With all my experience as a convict, I was filled with wonder that such barbarities could be committed in a civilized state without arousing a tempest of indignation. Yet they have existed for years and still exist."[1]

Indeed, it seemed as if the prevailing philosophy at the mines was simply to work the men to death and then replace them with more convicts. "If one dies, get another," someone once observed.

Shotwell reported that "It was almost an everyday occurrence for one or more men to be killed by coal falling from above, and when a poor unfortunate was killed and hoisted up out of the ground, the captain would sometimes say, 'Well, there's plenty more to take his place.'" For this "service," the H&TC Railroad was paying the state thirty-one dollars per month per convict.

Water seeping into the mines from the Brazos River was a constant problem, and the convicts were usually forced to stand ankle-deep in stagnant water while being required to mine seven tons of coal a day per man.

Just a few years after Shotwell's observations, the *Report of the Penitentiary Investigating Committee including All Exhibits and Testimony Taken by the Committee* reported the condition of the feet of the convicts working under these conditions:

> They are very dirty and have scales on them like an alligator's foot. They are wrinkled, scaly and cracked and have the appearance of being painted with iodine and the bottom is as black as a negro's foot. They are brown, parched and shriveled, the skin having the appearance of dead skin and are red up to and above the ankle.[2]

The water was an ever-present problem, affecting not only the health of the convicts but the profits of the railroad. One summer Shotwell was pulled from the mines with several other convicts to build a levee to hold the river water out of the mines. To get them back into the mines quicker, the guards forced them to work at an accelerated pace, causing several of the men to pass out from the heat, humidity, and exhaustion. When this happened, Shotwell alleges, the captain would order the convict stripped, laid out on the ground, and whipped bloody to "see if he was really unconscious."

Even appearing sick was avoided at the Calvert mines, Shotwell claims, because the ailing inmate would be ordered to gulp down a double plate of food in a short time. Failure to complete the task resulted in thirty-nine lashes with the bat and work the next day.[3]

Surprisingly, Shotwell, who was particularly critical of the prison system in all aspects, reported, "...the food, bedding and sanitary conditions were reasonably good, but the rest was h—l on earth."

This observation is particularly surprising given the other reports of terrible living conditions. The 1910 legislative investigating committee report documented the following encounter with one of the convicts at Calvert:

He has no underwear. Just two top [outer] pieces. Coat or shirt may have been washed a couple of years ago. Has no button nor button holes either in front or on the sleeves. Greasy black in appearance. All stripes obliterated by reason of the dirty grease, etc. Trousers black in appearance and dirty, greasy and smutty, without any buttons. Fastened around the waist with a horseshoe nail, without belt or suspenders. Too large in the waist by six or eight inches or more. Sleeves of the shirt without buttons and are ragged. Shirt fastened in front with a match. Both shirt and trousers decidedly filthy.[4]

Concluding that the Calvert lignite mines were, even by the terrible standards found throughout the convict lease camps, disgusting, unsanitary, and brutal, the committee report recommended, "...in our judgment this contract, which has been renewed for two years from January 1, 1910, should be cancelled at once."[5]

---

1   Shotwell, John, *A Victim of Revenge or Fourteen Years in Hell*, pg. 18.

2   *Report of the Penitentiary Investigating Committee including All Exhibits and Testimony Taken by the Committee*, pp. 613-616 quoted from *Penology for Profit, A History of the Texas Prison System 1867-1912*, by Donald R. Walker, pg. 137.

3   *Report of the Penitentiary Investigating Committee including All Exhibits and Testimony Taken by the Committee*, pp. 18-19.

4   Ibid., 613-616, quoted from *Penology for Profit, A History of the Texas Prison System 1867-1912*, pg. 137.

5   Ibid., pg. 13.

Chapter Eighteen

Why the Aggies are Hated in Texas Prisons

While white and Mexican inmates were often leased to sawmill squads, railroad crews, or coal mines, the agricultural leases tended to use African-American convicts predominantly. This work was continued year round. It involved chopping and breaking the soil in the crop rows, thinning the plants, weeding the rows, and finally, picking the crops—usually cotton. In between there were other chores such as clearing fence lines and cleaning irrigation ditches.

The rule of silence was usually enforced in the fields, but some bosses would allow singing, and the squads would sometimes talk back and forth to each other in singsong verses. Shortly after the lease system had officially ended, Huddie Ledbetter (better known as Leadbelly) worked the fields of the Sugar Land unit and recalled that those singsong verses inspired much of his later critically acclaimed music. But usually it was silence that followed the hoe squads, punctuated only by the sound of the hoes rhythmically breaking the crust of the soil.

But some decade before Leadbelly arrived at Sugar Land, the unit was used by Texas as a farm for incorrigible white inmates. Bill Mills recalled that he was transferred to the Imperial Farm at Sugar Land on June 9, 1915:

> When we arrived the land had just got dry enough to work after a flood. Cotton was about 18 inches high and Johnson grass about twice as high. As I was an ex-convict they put me in No. 1 hoe squad the first morning. The prison hoe is known as "one-eyed Aggie." It is not like the hoe used by free citizens. It is a big solid piece of steel weighing from one to two pounds. The handle is made of sassafras sprouts with the bark not taken off. Of course, from time to time each prisoner would try to smooth his own hoe handle.[1]

Aggies are not lightweight little garden tools such as a weekend gardener would use. They are heavy-duty and over-sized instruments designed to break the ground with every strike. Over the decades, they have also broken many inmates as well.

The field force was divided into "hoe squads" of up to twenty-five inmates each. In later years the hoe squads would leave the main unit or camp and ride on wagons to the area of the fields in which they would be working that day. During the lease period, however, the leased convicts would be expected to walk or run up to several miles to the fields and back daily. The field bosses would ride their horses hard on the convicts' heels, sometimes running a slow inmate down beneath the horse's sharp hooves. Other times the bosses would ride close behind and whip the inmates.

Once at the site of the needed work, the squads would march down the turn row, the area between fields where the plow or other equipment could turn around to start back down the subsequent rows. Each inmate would choose a row and line up in it waiting for the order to start.

"Ketch in" meant for each inmate to get a row and start working it with the hoe. They would hack the dirt and pulverize it. This aerated the soil and cleared weeds. Other times the field boss would start the squad moving with the order to "blacken them rows!"

As the crop was just starting to show through the soil, the hoe squads would be ordered to go down the rows and leave "four stalks to a hill." This meant thinning the row and leaving four cotton stalks in a cluster a hoe blade apart. An experienced convict could hit the exact spots time after time, and hoe squads would get into a rhythm in which the aggies were rising and falling in a synchronized pattern. It was claimed a good field boss could tell if somebody was lagging just by listening to the rhythmic sound of the blades hitting the soil.

One inmate, usually the fastest, would be assigned as "lead hoe" and would set the pace, and all the rest of the hoe squad would be expected to keep up but slightly behind the lead hoe. He would be monitored closely by the mounted field boss and be expected to motivate or challenge any of his squad members who didn't keep up. In clay gumbo soil, the squads would often work up a row chopping one side and then return the same row working the other side.

The Texas prison system today has been mechanized. Large numbers of convicts in hoe squads are seldom seen in the prison fields, and those squads that do turn out do not work the backbreaking speed of the lease years. Today's hoe squads ride on tractor-pulled wagons to and from the fields and even have portable latrine facilities. The hours are closely monitored today, and weather conditions are strictly defined as to when the convict members of the squad may turn out.

But during the lease period system of the 1800s and early 1900s, hoe squads grabbed their aggies and ran several miles to the fields regardless of the weather conditions. Once there, they worked from "can to can't"—when the field boss "can see" to when he "can't see." In other words, they worked from sunup to sundown. Then they would run several miles back to the camp in the dusk to be shuffled through a meal of "ol' hog and bread."

The lucky ones had rough, poorly constructed brogan boots that tore their feet apart. The unlucky ones worked the fields barefooted.

Working this schedule throughout the year—but especially during the summer growing months—the convicts would usually be allowed to bathe once a week, on Saturday nights. Usually they weren't given a change of clothing but simply put their filthy work clothes back on afterwards. Bathing facilities consisted typically of a concrete trough, and up to a hundred men would use the same water and be handed a piece of rough Osnaburg cloth—similar to a cheap grade of denim—to use as a towel. Many times all one hundred men would use only one piece of cloth.

And throughout all this, the root of their evil—the instrument of their greatest torture in the fields—was the "aggie." To a man, it can be said the convicts of that period hated aggies with a vengeance.

---

1   Mills, Bill, *25 Years Behind Prison Bars*, pp. 26-27.

Chapter Nineteen

(1910-1938)

25 Years Behind Prison Bars

The Texas Prison Memoir of Bill Mills

A man was supposed to be in the dark cell thirty-six hours. Therefore, to keep the prisoners in the fields, they would punish as many as possible from Saturday night to Monday morning. The dark cell usually was full of men from 8 o'clock Saturday night until Monday morning, with only one cup of water and one piece of corn bread Sunday at noon. The dark cell was a wooden room about eight feet long, six feet wide, and six feet high. It had no bedding or anything in it, so the prisoner was undressed and pushed in there without anything except a gown. They had to sleep on the floor unless there were too many to lie down. I have seen as many as eight men in a cell at one time for thirty-six hours.

Bill Mills served seven sentences in prison, five of them in Texas, for a total of twenty-five years during the period 1910 to 1938. Like many other ex-convict diarists, Mills dedicates his memoirs to "preventing some young man from leading a life of crime."

Mills' perspective of prison life in Texas, however, is unique in that his many years behind prison bars included time during the convict lease period, the subsequent era of state-operated prison farms, and during the early years of the first true prison reformation efforts in the early 1930s.

Another element that makes his narrative, titled *25 Years Behind Prison Bars*, unusual is that during the many years he served in Texas prisons, he was assigned to virtually every prison farm in Texas at one time. Through *25 Years Behind Prison Bars*, he gives us descriptions and accounts of serving prison time throughout the system including many work farms that are no longer in existence.

His first sentence in Texas prisons was imposed when he was seventeen years old, following what had been an early introduction to the criminal lifestyle as a runaway working in East Texas sawmills and for traveling carnivals.

He was born on August 28, 1893, on a farm in Rains County, Texas. His severe stuttering problem kept him out of school most of his childhood, and forced to do hard farm labor as a child, he began running away from home at a very early age. Through his association with often itinerant sawmill workers and traveling carnival workers, he began cheating and stealing before he had become a teenager.

Ten days after his seventeenth birthday, he was arrested in Hunt County for horse theft, convicted, and sentenced to two years in prison.

On December 4, 1910, prison transfer agent Bud Russell picked up Mills and thirteen other prisoners. They were paired, a short chain attached from neck to neck of each pair, and a long chain locked on the front couple, extended to the pair of inmates in the back.

Mills, possibly because of his young age, recalled he was particularly humiliated by this ritual when they were marched out of the jail and forced to shuffle up the center of the street, like yoked animals, as the local townspeople watched.

They boarded a train car and were transported to Fort Worth then transferred to a train for Cleburne, Texas, and there they spent the night in the city jail. During that first day Mills violated a prison transfer rule by sticking his head out of the train window to talk to a girl at a station platform—an action that resulted in a threat that he would be shot.

The next morning they boarded another train to the Hill County State Farm near Blum, known then as the Burleson and John Farm. The final stage of the trip from Blum to the prison unit involved a ride on an open wagon during a Texas blue norther in which the temperature dropped and the wind picked up, making the exposed inmates miserable. Mills recalled he was almost glad to arrive at the prison farm.

At the Burleson and John Farm, he became Texas Inmate #37538 and immediately received his second threat of being shot. Upon arriving at the farm, he was so anxious to have his neck chains removed that he ran up to the guard who had the key, causing the other guards to draw their rifles on him.

The Burleson and John Farm was a three-thousand-acre state-run prison farm located on the Brazos River. The prison unit was what the inmates referred to as a cotton-picking farm and was so large the boundaries spanned into Hill and Bosque Counties.

Immediately upon arrival, Mills and the other new prisoners were stripped, issued striped prison uniforms, and given a crude pair of brogan boots with no socks. At the time, Mills thought the boots were in such bad condition they were useless.

Very quickly, however, he would realize how fortunate he was to get any footwear upon arrival; at many other prison farms, inmates were working the fields barefoot.

Once deloused, shaved, and issued prison clothing, he was given his first prison meal and quickly indoctrinated in proper "prison dining etiquette."

> The prisoners were not allowed to speak a word in the dining room. We used signs instead of speaking. If we wanted something served in our plates we held the plate up.

He quickly learned that prison breakfasts consisted of biscuits or corn bread with syrup and flour gravy and little else. Lunch typically consisted of corn bread and one piece of boiled meat at the Burleson and John Farm. Sometimes, during the gardening months, peas, turnip greens, and occasionally potatoes would be available, but only if the food steward chose to include them. Supper would almost always be a repeat of the dinner menu, often consisting of cold leftovers from midday.

The three thousand acres of prison crops were tended by a relatively small number of inmates who lived in two main buildings. One, known as the "single building," was built like a barn with a picket office at one end where the guard watched over the prisoners. The other building was twice as large and known simply as the "double building"; it had a guard's picket office in the center with rows of sleeping quarters along both sides—a living quarters concept still used in Texas prisons today.

Beds consisted of wooden slat bunks built three high and supplied with corn shuck mattresses. As a newly assigned inmate, Mills was told to find a top bunk. His first night in prison he was assigned the sleeping quarters and mattress of an inmate who had just died in the bunk as the result of a beating.

In 1910 there were no Texas laws regulating the work schedules of prisoners, and Mills quickly learned that work days on the state farms extended from daylight to dark.

He was assigned to a field squad during cotton-picking season and was immediately required to pick three hundred pounds per day, a quota difficult for experienced inmate field hands. Mills, who had spent the previous months lying around in a county jail cell, struggled to make his daily quota. The guards had no sympathy for his physical conditioning and immediately threatened him with a beating if he failed to produce his three-hundred-pound quota.

Somehow he managed, but on the second day in the field, he claims he and his work squad were forced to witness a beating of an inmate who had failed to pick his quota of cotton. It was Mills' introduction to the dreaded bat.

As part of the overall punishment strategy, prison officials required other inmates to hold the convict being punished while the strap was applied to his back. Because he was new to the farm, Mills was one of the inmates instructed to help hold the inmate selected for the beating. He relates the effect the strapping had on him:

> We laid him on his stomach, pulled his pants down to his knees, baring the skin, and his shirt was pulled up under his arms. Two men held each of his legs, one man on each arm and one astraddle of his head, which happened to be I, in the present instance, because it was the captain's command. I think he wanted to put a scare into me, and he succeeded.

By 1910 Texas state law had reduced the number of blows an inmate could be given from thirty-nine to a maximum of twenty, although Mills claimed the punishing officials often ignored the new regulation.

On this occasion, Mills was assigned the job of holding the punished inmate's head and was literally sitting on him, forcing his face into the ground as he screamed under the pain of the blows. When the captain warned him to stifle the screams, Mills bore down on the inmate's head until he buried his nose and mouth in the sand and nearly smothered him.

The twenty lashes, Mills claims, were spread out over an eight to twelve-minute time span to increase the pain between blows. "The first few licks caused very red spots but by the time the last lash is put on," he recalled, "it is a solid blister which looks bluish black."

Then, because he was new to the squad, the captain made him smell the sweaty and bloody bat as a warning that he would be next if he failed to pick his allotted share in the fields.

He survived those early days and avoided a beating throughout the remainder of the cotton season. On Christmas that year the field workers were given the day off work—not necessarily a luxury enjoyed throughout the prison system. Lunch was the same fare as any other work day on that first Christmas, except that one piece of apple pie was included to celebrate the holiday.

In January 1911 the inmates were given new uniforms, without stripes, and informed they would be earning ten cents per day for every day served. That law would later be abolished and never reinstated in Texas.

On July 21, 1911, Bill Mills received an unexpected conditional pardon and was released from prison. After serving eight months of a two-year sentence, he was discharged back into society. He was an eighteen-year-old kid with no education, a prison record, and what should have been a crime-ending education in the brutality of Texas prison work farms.

It wasn't. Shortly after returning to Emory, Texas, he was in trouble again and fled the county in what would become a year-long drinking spree through Texas, Kansas, and ending in Oklahoma when he was arrested and sentenced to a year in prison at McAlester.

He discharged on April 21, 1914, and was arrested in Wichita Falls, Texas, three days later on an outstanding bootlegging charge. He eventually was tried and found not guilty, but he had embarked on a life of crime and imprisonment that would last for another two decades.

In the fall of 1914 he was convicted of a firearms charge and sentenced to another five years in the Texas prison system. This time he was sent to Huntsville in May of 1915, and he recalls those five years as "hell on earth" and more cruel and inhuman than any other prison unit he would serve time on during the next twenty years.

Despite being the central headquarters prison unit in Texas, the Huntsville unit had terrible food, and Mills found the sanitation and living conditions were worse than on the Burleson and John Farm.

Inside the massive brick walls at Huntsville, he was assigned to a two-man cell instead of the dormitory-type living quarters he had known at the farm unit. The cells had no running water and only two buckets—one for drinking water and one to be used as a commode.

While at Huntsville he was assigned to saw wood in the lower yard near the boiler room, a job he held until he was transferred to the Imperial Farm at Sugar Land on June 9, 1915. There, he was assigned to a hoe squad chopping Johnson grass out of the cotton rows.

Again Mills found himself on a prison farm unit with a grueling work quota after having spent the previous eight months sitting in a jail cell. His first day on the squad, the crew walked three miles to the fields at a brisk pace and then spent the day hoeing grass before walking the three miles back in the evening.

At Sugar Land, Mills quickly learned, this was considered a typical field schedule of sixteen hours per day. Imperial Farm field bosses used to brag: "We work 'em eight-hour days—eight in the morning and eight in the afternoon."

Mills suffered greatly those first days on the hoe squad and received no sympathy from the guards or the other inmates. His back sore and his hands raw and bloody from hoeing all day, he requested medical attention. When the guards denied his request, some of the other inmates suggested he report to the prison hospital for some "lightning oil" to put on his back.

It turned out to be a cruel hoax, and the "lightning oil," whatever it was, burned and irritated his skin so badly he was unable to sleep that night. As the guards and other inmates laughed at his predicament, he was allowed to visit a stock tank several times that night and soaked in the water to relieve the burning. The next morning he was told to report to his squad, without any sleep or rest, and work another sixteen-hour day.

Again he managed to survive those first two days, and on the third day at Imperial he was assigned to a plow squad, which was considered a desirable job during certain seasons but a "death sentence" at others—especially after heavy rains. Mills claims that over time, he watched men being worked behind the plows until they dropped in the hot sun, some dying of heatstroke. "Mules cost money—men don't," the field bosses would tell them, and Mills claims that the mules were, in fact, treated much better than the inmates.

Although he was able to adapt quickly to the requirements of the work squad in the field, Mills did not escape the dark cell or the bat.

His first major punishment was for fighting with another inmate. That infraction resulted in his being thrown into the dark cell for thirty-six hours. The cell, he recalled, was six feet by eight feet with a six-foot ceiling and had nothing inside it.

"Mules cost money, men don't," Bill Mills claimed field bosses told inmates during the convict lease system. Mules were used in Texas prisons into the 1950s, and many convict memoirs recall the animals being treated better than the inmates who utilized them. Photo source: Texas State Archives, courtesy of Jester III unit, Texas Department of Criminal Justice.

He was stripped, given a thin frock much like a hospital gown, and forced to sleep on the concrete floor. During those thirty-six hours, he was given one cup of water and one piece of corn bread.

As severe as assignment to the dark cell would seem, its use was seen by prison officials as the first warning prior to subsequent punishments by the bat. Once Mills had received his first warning in that darkened cell, his later punishments amounted to beatings at the hands of the guards.

Bill Mills claims he was later punished three more times for "whispering too loudly in the building."

In 1915 he was sent to the nearby Harlem Farm, where he worked at "sugar rolling," or cutting sugarcane. A year later, back at the Imperial Farm, he was caught talking to another inmate in the cotton fields and assigned a quota of picking six hundred pounds that day. He claims he weighed in at the end of the day with 597 pounds and as a result was held down and whipped for laziness.

Mills, in *25 Years Behind Prison Bars*, details a rare account almost never reported in prison—a guard revolt. It was at the Imperial Farm in July of 1917 that a new captain was assigned from the Walls unit in Huntsville to take charge of the work squads. The captain became known as "Pistol Pete" and would remain at Imperial from July 1 to September 10 of 1917.

During that period, administration of a strapping or use of the bat had at least some institutional regulation with regards to the number of lashes and a prohibition against the striking on bloody areas of the body. Almost every inmate narrative describing the use of the leather instrument suggested prison rules were routinely ignored.

But the new Imperial Farm captain, Pistol Pete, completely disregarded the rules and rewrote his own set of punishment standards, according to Mills. Using a six-foot bullwhip, which was absolutely banned, he would ride among the field crews,

Undated photograph showing inmates working sugarcane cranes—possibly at the Imperial unit near Sugar Land. Photo source: Texas State Archives

Inmates working sugarcane fields. Photo source, Texas State Archives

lashing out at any nearby inmate whether that convict was picking his quota or not. Each day, as a result, several inmates would be carried to the hospital on the water wagon to be treated for the severe cuts and welts on their backs.

Each field squad of inmates had a mounted guard supervising it at all times, and Mills recalls that on September 10 Pistol Pete began lashing workers in one of the squads when the field boss in charge of it drew his pistol and threatened to kill the captain if he lashed any inmate one more time.

When the captain coiled his whip, the field boss announced he was quitting rather than witness any more of the cruelty in the fields. The captain attempted to assign another field guard to supervise that squad, but no other officer would accept the job and each, in turn, submitted his resignation also.

When the crews returned to the Imperial Farm at the end of that workday, the sheriff and prosecuting attorney from Fort Bend County, as well as commissioners from Huntsville, greeted Pistol Pete.

Inside the prison hospital they had found thirty-eight inmates admitted for whip wounds. As a result, they filed thirty-eight misdemeanor charges on the captain and fired him.

25 Years Behind Prison Bars is one of the very few accounts of early Texas prison history in which guards are reported to have revolted. To defy a field captain was something unheard of, and if it did ever occur, the incident was something kept hidden from the inmates and the public.

According to Mills, Pistol Pete later plea-bargained to have the charges dropped in return for a promise never to work for the prison system again. But conditions at Imperial improved dramatically after that incident, and Mills states that he finished his sentence there with little trouble.

Early 1900s photograph of an unnamed "field boss" on one of the state prison farm units. Photo source, Texas State Archives

He continued to have troubles with the law, however, after his release from prison. He was arrested immediately upon discharge and was charged with auto theft but was eventually acquitted. He managed to successfully defend against charges of postal robbery in Dallas, but his luck ran out in 1921.

He was convicted in Wise County and sentenced to forty-eight years in prison. Mills does not specify what the offense was that time, but two days later he was also convicted in Emory, Texas, with an additional two-year sentence, giving him a combined fifty years to serve in a prison cell.

By 1921 the convict lease system had been abolished in Texas, at least "officially." Many of the former lease camps had simply been converted in to state-run prison work farms, but *25 Years Behind Prison Bars* was one of the rare narratives in which the conditions were reported to have improved considerably while the brutality and torture were reduced.

Mills began doing his own legal appeals and succeeded in getting his sentence reduced to two years. Before his discharge on this greatly reduced sentence, however, he also learned how to make bogus money and quickly applied his newfound skills after leaving prison.

Counterfeiting is a federal crime, and after his arrest on those charges, Mill was convicted and sentenced to two years in federal prison in 1924.

Compared to Texas prisons, he claims, the federal penitentiary was almost a country club. He also discharged that sentence, returned to Houston, and married a schoolteacher in 1926.

It would appear that after several convictions and prison sentences, Bill Mills had finally succeeded in giving his life some positive direction. He started a family in Houston and claimed he was the "happiest man on the earth."

But prior to his marriage, his life had been a cycle of lawlessness punctuated by arrests, convictions, prison time, discharge, and continuing lawlessness. After six months of his "heaven on earth" as a married man in Houston, Bill Mills was arrested again, this time in Denton, and was sentenced to yet another tour in Texas prison—for four additional years.

From 1927 until his discharge in 1930, Mills was assigned to various jobs on the Blakely Farm, the Walls unit in Huntsville, the Ferguson Farm, the Clemens Farm, and finally at Huntsville again. He discharged on February 24, 1930.

He lasted nearly a year on the "outside" this time before being convicted and sentenced on December 22 to another twelve-year term for robbery with firearms.

Mills was processed into the Huntsville unit on June 26, 1931, and was immediately sent to the infamous Eastham Farm, the only prison unit in Texas on which he had not served prior time. Eastham was a hardened work farm, reserved for the worst of the repeating violent offenders. While assigned there, Mills met and lived with violent outlaws such as Clyde Barrow, Joe Palmer, and Raymond Hamilton.

After a short period at Eastham, he was transferred to the Harlem Farm, then back to the Walls unit at Huntsville, and finally to the Wynne Farm. At Wynne, in 1935, he was classified as a "knock-out," a derogatory term describing an inmate who was too physically broken down to work.

While nothing else in his life seemed to have effectively stopped his criminal behavior, age and infirmity seemed to have finally signaled the need for him to reform.

He discharged the Texas prison system for the final time on July 25, 1938, based upon good behavior. While at the Wynne unit he had converted to Christianity, and in the years following his release he did appear to evangelize his new-found spirituality by traveling around the state and lecturing at-risk youth about the horrors of prison time.

25 Years Behind Prison Bars is thought to have been published in 1939, a year after his final release from prison. It was updated at least once, in 1951, and Mills appears to have used the booklet as a genuine, no-holds-barred approach to influencing young people.

He dedicated his post-incarceration years to delivering over 4,000 lectures to the public, promoting his "Crime Does Not Pay" program for youth.

25 Years Behind Prison Bars is also unique in that, in it, Bill Mills portrays a Texas prison system through nearly three decades of almost continuous personal incarceration over a period spanning three distinct eras of criminal justice practice. His first sentences were served during the final years of the convict lease system, but he also served time in Texas prisons during the period of the state-operated work farms, and in his final years of incarceration he did "hard time" during the period of legislative-mandated reform under Texas prison general manager, Lee Simmons.

Bill Mills published his prison memoirs around 1939 and became an advocate working with young people to keep them from following his criminal example. The booklet was reprinted at least once, in 1951, and was widely distributed to young men on his lecture circuits. Here, in the introduction, he offers a photo after his final release from prison in 1938.
Mills, Bill, *25 Years Behind Prison Bars* (Emory, TX: No publisher listed, 1939?)

A few passages can be found in *25 Years Behind Prison Bars* in which Bill Mills appears to be venting his frustration and resentment toward the Texas prison system. For the most part, however, he readily accepts responsibility for his actions and crimes and uses the booklet as a tool to inform and motivate.

The length of his total sentences and his widespread assignments throughout the Texas prison system make *25 Years Behind Prison Bars* a unique and valuable mirror of early twentieth-century Texas prisons.

Chapter Twenty

Tools of Torture

To a man, all of the ex-convicts writing their recollections of their time in Texas prisons from the 1870s to the 1920s detailed the systems of punishment they or inmates around them were subjected to. Much of what they describe does, in fact, suggest a "Texas Gulag" or even a "Texas Inquisition," especially during the period of the convict lease system.

And while it's necessary to remember that these men certainly had "axes to grind" in their memoirs, it is also true that many outside agencies and groups, including the Texas legislature, also reported these cruel and unusual punishments.

Without question, the bat was the most common method of punishment described in detail by the former prisoners. But the bat was only one of many forms of punishment that prison officials and guards used during this period.

Ironically, the "ball and chain" was seldom mentioned. Andrew L. George, writing of the period of 1885-1891, recalled that convicts "...are required to wear while at work a ball and chain. The chain is about three and a half feet long with a ball weighing two to five pounds at one end; at the other end is an iron band that goes on the ankle, which a blacksmith rivets on and which cannot be taken off until the blacksmith service is again sought. Wearing this annoying and cumbersome apparatus they are required to do a big task of labor daily."[1]

John Dunn, also during the 1880s, recalled the prisoners in the lease camps being chained with a ball. The inmates, he claimed, had chains locked around their ankles and despite any precaution taken, the chains and ankle clamps rubbed the skin raw, making it difficult to walk because the chains were expected to drag the ground. Only when the guards granted permission were inmates allowed to pick up the ball and chain completely from the ground.[2]

This 2½ pound ball and chain on display at the Texas Prison Museum was only one of many punishments inmates under the convict lease system were subjected to.
Photo by Gary Brown, courtesy of the Texas Prison Museum

Chains, however, were used extensively in other forms of punishment, usually involving the inmates hanging from something.

Beecher Deason, writing of the 1920s, listed this as one of the forms of punishment he witnessed: "Another was the chains, or a singletree hung upon a chain or rope. An unruly prisoner would be hung up by his wrists and pulled up until his toes alone touched the floor. I have seen men so stubborn they would hang on the chains until they swooned and became unconscious before they would give up."[3]

Another inmate during that period, Bill Mills, also recalled, "They would hang a man by his wrists. This was done by putting a small block and tackle in the ceiling of the building with a long rope running through it, extending downward. Another chain or piece of leather would extend from that to a man's wrist. At command of the picket guard, the building tender fastened this to a prisoner's wrist, then the picket guard would pull the rope until he got the prisoner on tip toes. And it wasn't unusual to swing him clear off the floor. According to the rules he was supposed to hang three or four hours. But that depended on whether or not he became unconscious."[4]

Hanging by chains, however, dated back to the very earliest of the memoirs. Henry Tomlin wrote of being punished by "...my hands cuffed together and fastened to the ceiling of the cell. In this way I would stand until my legs would give out and then I would fall down and swing by my wrists."[5]

Charles Favor likewise recalled a similar punishment, "Standing on the alley, or hanging in the window, is very tiresome and straining on the muscles, as certain muscles only are exercised. I've seen men stand on the alley or hang on the window until they looked like they would drop dead."[6]

"Standing on the alley" involved an inmate being hung by his wrists until he could only touch the ground by standing on his tiptoes. This was usually done in the hallway so other inmates would be required to walk by and observe the punishment—hence the expression "alley."

Charles Favor gives this sketch of an inmate being chained to his cell bars. Various narratives listed this as a common punishment in the late 1800s. The inmate's wrists would be chained to the bars at a height that his feet could not touch the floor—forcing him to either hang or draw his feet up and relieve his body weight which, in turn, caused severe leg cramps. Favor, Charles A., *Twenty-Two Months in the Texas Penitentiary* (Corsicana, TX: Democrat Print, 1900).

"Hanging in the window" was a technique in which the inmate would be chained by the wrists to the very top of a barred window—high enough that he would be required to pull his feet up and rest them on one of the crossbars. This would place him in a squatting position off the floor but suspended by the weight of his body on the wrist chains.

Both the alley and window punishments were designed to require only certain muscles be exercised and therefore would cause extreme cramping and fatigue.

Favor also recalled his own experience with being chained: "I was chained up for two months...I had to stand chained there twelve hours each day deprived of everything that might bring hope to my breast...."[7]

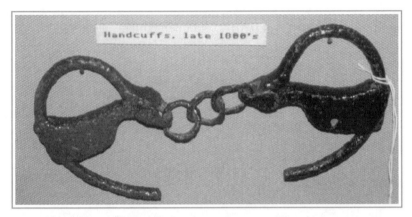

These handcuffs, dated late-1880s, were the type used to restrain inmates during the convict lease period. They were almost always used in conjunction with neck chains and/or leg chains. Photo by Gary Brown, courtesy of the Texas Prison Museum

J.S. Calvin, writing of the threat facing inmates in the 1890s, claimed of the prison captain, "You see he could punish them by chaining them up, by hanging them in the window, or by making them stand on the floor until 2 o'clock at night."[8]

At least two former inmates recalled the use of the "spur" to prevent troublesome inmates making an attempt to escape from the work camps. "The spur," according to Andrew

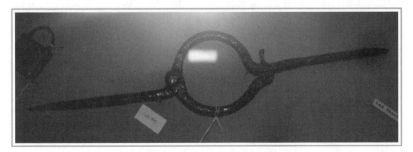

This is the infamous "spur" which was attached to the ankle. The spur allowed an inmate to function on a work crew but severely limited his ability to walk fast or run. It was usually used as a punishment after a failed escape attempt. Photo by Gary Brown, courtesy of the Texas Prison Museum

George, "consisted of two sharpened spikes attached to an iron band" and effectively prevented an escaping convict making any speed at running.[9]

Charles Favor also described the spur as "...an iron contrivance made to fit closely around the ankle, and projects some eight or ten inches behind and in front. The man who is 'spurred' cannot run fast. He must, however, do the same amount of labor, which makes it very difficult."[10]

In the 1920s prison officials used a punishment tool referred to variously as the "pole" or the "carpenter horse." Mills described it as "...a rough pole, some with sharp edges, put up in the building. A man had to sit astraddle this pole for several hours."[11]

Designed with the bevel upward so the inmate had to sit astride it with the sharpened edge between his legs, the victim would have to suffer the effects of his body weight forcing him down on the pole. Deason, from another unit, described a similar device, "One was similar to a carpenter horse. Just high enough off the floor so sitting astride of it his feet would not touch the floor. It was called the 'pole'."[12]

Another pamphlet published during the 1920s described this punishment. *It's Hell in a Texas Pen* was a collection of undocumented inmate claims but did describe the tool Deason and Mills referred to: "This horse is a beveled scantling about six feet from the floor. I have seen many a poor devil ride this pole from early in the evening until 12 o'clock at night, without a bite to eat or drink. Some of these poor fellows could not put on their shoes the next morning for their swollen feet."[13]

It's Hell in a Texas Pen also reported a variation of "chain hanging" allegedly used at the Retrieve unit in the 1920s in which a Negro convict was subject to being "...hung up on a 'ladder' by his hands, his feet not touching the floor, and the palms of his hands were bursted open."[14]

Solitary confinement, or the "hole," has traditionally been a punishment used for the more severe cases of inmate misconduct. From the 1890s through the 1920s, however, it was usually referred to as the dark cell.

Of another inmate, Charles Campbell recalled, "Therefore they hit him thirty-nine more lashes and dragged him to the dark cell, which is a frightful, foul-smelling dungeon almost air tight and painted jet black inside. The blackness of this hole is positively painful. Not even the faintest ray of light is ever discernable—nothing but complete, horrible darkness."[15]

Charles Favor, like Campbell, was at the Rusk prison in the 1890s and similarly recalls, "It is a solid cell with no ventilation at all. When the unfortunate who gets in there is on the inside, the heavy iron door is closed and then it is dark as a dungeon and but little to eat and drink...there was nothing on the floor—rock—except an old worn out quilt. I begun to perspire in great drops, and soon I wanted water. I felt something biting me and I ascertained that it was chintzes—the largest and most ferocious ones I ever saw. I never was so tormented in my life."[16]

Another form of physical punishment, and one used by the Texas prisons until the 1980s, was that of being forced to stand on a barrel at night. Over the years variations of the barrel were used—milk crates, Coke crates, and oil drums—but the practice started in the 1800s with the use of wooden barrels. The inmate being punished would be placed atop the barrel in a conspicuous place, usually the center hall, and made to stand there, sometimes all night before going back to work the next day. The object was to bring about leg cramps, and if the inmate stepped off or fell off, his assigned time on the barrel would start over. Both Deason and Mills give descriptions of the barrel in their narratives.[17]

Other forms of punishment or torture were reported by several of the former inmates. One of the bitterest recollections was provided by Henry Tomlin who claimed, "They blistered my back with Spanish flies and painted it with iodine and probed me as if they were trying to find out what was the matter."[18]

Other reports claimed prison officials forced inmates to "...carry a green Elm log with the rough bark on, weighing from 100 to 150 pounds, on their shoulders until they drop."[19]

Still other allegations, unsubstantiated, claimed prison guards forced inmates to climb ant-infested trees as punishment or would order them held naked over ant beds by other inmates.

While many of these claims of barbaric and sadistic treatment by the guards were undocumented, it is also true that gross mistreatment of the inmates including some of these very techniques were also uncovered and well documented.

The legislative committee members visiting the prisons and camps in the preparation of the 1910 *Report of the Penitentiary Investigating Committee* uncovered terrible allegations of mistreatment including the severe whipping of a fourteen-year-old boy for possession of matches.[20]

Even more disturbing were reports that guards would force inmates to perform disgusting, even perverted acts for their own entertainment. The 1910 report alleges one sergeant forced a convict to dance on the wooden coffin of a recently deceased inmate in one of the camps.[21] That same sergeant, it was claimed, also forced an inmate to eat his own feces on the Whatley Farm.[22]

At Clemens Camp #2, committee members were informed that two Negro inmates had been caught playing "man and wife" in the barracks. Their punishment, several inmates testified, was to each be strapped with the bat and then forced to lick each other's anus.[23]

Without question, Texas penitentiaries and work camps during the period of the 1880s through the early 1900s were places of "hard time."

1   George, Andrew L., *The Texas Convict: Sketches of the Penitentiary, Convict Farms and Railroads, Together with Poems*, pg. 7.
2   Evans, Max, *Long John Dunn of Taos, From Texas Outlaw to New Mexico Hero*, pp. 48-49.
3   Deason, Beecher, *Seven Years in Texas Prisons*, pg. 5.
4   Mills, Bill, *25 Years Behind Prison Bars*, pg. 29.
5   Tomlin, Henry, *Henry Tomlin, the man who fought the brutality and oppression of the ring in the state of Texas for eighteen years and won. The story of how men traffic in the liberties and lives of their fellow men*, pg. 39.
6   Favor, Charles A., *Twenty-Two Months in the Texas Penitentiary*, pg. 61.
7   Ibid., pg. 120.
8   Calvin, J.S., *Buried alive, or, A term in the Texas State Prison, 1898-1902: a chapter from real life*, pg. 71.
9   George, pg. 7.
10 Favor, pg. 26.
11 Mills, pg. 41.
12 Deason, pg. 5.
13 *It's Hell in a Texas Pen, the barbarous conditions as told by ex-convicts and unearthed by the Legislature* (Dallas?: 1925?), pamphlet on file at the Center for American History, University of Texas at Austin. pg. 12.
14 Ibid., pg. 38.
15 Ibid., pg. 20.
16 Favor, pg. 61.
17 Deason, pg. 5 and Mills, pg. 51.
18 Tomlin, pg. 38.
19 *It's Hell in a Texas Pen*, pg. 11.
20 *Report of the Penitentiary Investigating Committee including All Exhibits and Testimony Taken by the Committee*, pg. 245.
21 Ibid., pg. 254.
22 Ibid., pg. 256.
23 Ibid., pp. 918-919.

Chapter Twenty-One

(Late 1890s)

Hell Exploded

The Texas Prison Memoir
of Charles C. Campbell

By the time they quit working that evening the palms of my hands were a solid blister, and the next morning, when I applied to an official for permission to go to the hospital to get something to alleviate the pain, he replied that he would give me a good remedy after breakfast, which proved to be a rusty crow-bar and a rough handled pick on the ore beds. I saw that there was no alternative but to work and suffer torture, so I went at it, and within ten minutes the entire insides of my hands were as devoid of skin as a beefsteak, and the tools with which I had been working were red with blood.

During the late 1890s (the exact date is not specified) a new inmate arrived at the Rusk penitentiary who did not blend in with the other arrivals. He had an attitude problem, a chip on his shoulder, and appeared unimpressed with the brutal reputation of the Texas prison system and the Rusk unit in particular.

Prison officials and guards were accustomed to greeting new prisoners as they arrived, marching in lines, from the train station in town. Chained together by their necks and their legs, the newly sentenced convicts would shuffle awkwardly and attempt to coordinate steps and ankle chains as they arrived at the stone gate of the prison.

While returning ex-convicts often had a resigned or defeated look in their eyes during processing, the first-time inmates usually displayed a fear their eyes, body mannerisms, and speech could not hide.

But the new inmate arriving that day in the late 1890s was different. He had a smart mouth and sharp tongue when speaking to judges, juries, and law enforcement officers, and his jail records indicated he sought out every opportunity to insult, confront, and ridicule those who controlled him.

The inmate's name was Charles Campbell, and the guards at Rusk that day must have smiled to themselves as he arrived for processing into the prison system with a two-year sentence.

The prison transfer agent probably had already told them Campbell had insulted the judge at his trial and referred to the jury members as "thick headed." At the train station in Kaufman, he had stopped on the platform to read a poem ridiculing the local citizens and thanking them for his neck chains, which he referred to as "the ties that bind us."

Rusk guards and prison administrators had, for the past fifteen years or so, effectively handled and broken every smart-mouthed tough guy who had been sent to them by Texas juries. Charles Campbell, they must have reasoned, would be no different once he disappeared inside those massive gates.

Inmate Charles Campbell arrived at Rusk that day intent on maintaining his cavalier attitude, but after a relatively short sentence of two years at Rusk, he later wrote of his experience as "a Hades with much longer streets...."

What Campbell encountered during those two short years included a prison system that nearly broke him down physically and mentally. His prison experience at Rusk "got his heart right," as prison guards liked to describe their techniques with inmates, but that experience did not soften his sharp tongue and left him a bitter man, who later described his incarceration as a descent into hell. His prison narrative, not surprisingly, was titled *Hell Exploded*.

Hell Exploded is almost completely devoid of specific dates —even the exact years of his prison time at Rusk are never specified. *Hell Exploded* lacks a publisher name or publication date; the only time reference is a statement that Campbell had applied for a copyright in 1900, so his time at Rusk is thought to have been in the 1890s.

But the institutional adjustment problems Campbell brought to Rusk had been developing since he was a child. He claimed his problems with authority began when he was fourteen years old, orphaned, and abandoned to fend for himself.

What he acknowledged in passing but failed to attribute his problems to was his confrontational and insulting style when dealing with judges, lawmen, prison guards, and fellow inmates. It was an aspect of his personality that led directly to his "descent into hell," and *Hell Exploded* was his attempt to get back at the system by exposing the barbarous cruelty and prison horrors he claims he experienced on various work gangs in the East Texas penitentiary at Rusk.

It was just east of Dallas, in the small town of Terrell, that he was arrested and charged with forgery of a check. After a night of saloon activities including drinking and succumbing to the dictates of "fair Morpheus" (probably morphine, commonly used among the criminal element in the latter part of the nineteenth century), he claims he awoke with a strange check in his shirt pocket and tried to cash it at the local bank.

After his arrest he was arraigned in the Terrell courtroom, and Campbell claims he told the judge "he couldn't pass a hat at a nigger collection meeting much less a sentence, and that he nor none of his greasy heelers had the nerve to shoot a frog."

This was rural Texas, and "frontier justice" still dictated how the judicial system worked in many of these rural areas. At Terrell, the bailiffs responded to Campbell's insult by effectively beating him into a bloody pulp, dragging him to the city jail, and locking him up over the weekend without food, water, or medical attention. Campbell claimed that another inmate released during that period raised a warning that the jailers were planning to kill their smart-mouthed prisoner, and the alert had resulted in his being transferred to Kaufman, where his actual trial took place.

Campbell had not learned to keep his mouth shut and his opinions to himself, and he "tried in a good many ways to prove to the thick-headed jury that I was an unfortunate victim of heartless designers, but they failed to see it that way, and decided that two years would help to develop my immature muscles and put an honest brown color on my skin."

Convicted and sentenced to two years in prison, he could never have guessed the extent to which the next two years would prove the jurists correct.

After his sentencing, the state contractor arrived to pick him up and deliver him to the state prison system. The reality of serving time in Texas penitentiaries during the final years of the 1890s still had not registered with Campbell. On the way to the train depot for transfer, he claims, he composed a farewell address to the court and the citizens of Kaufman based upon the neck chains he and the other prisoners were wearing. That poem, titled "The Ties That Bind Us," referred to the Kaufman locals as free lunch fiends and human velocipedes, and sarcastically thanked them for maintaining "ties" with the prisoners through the use of the neck chains.

From Kaufman, still wearing "the ties that bind," he and the other prisoners were transferred to Tyler in a boxcar and forced to spend the night sleeping inside it, still wearing their neck chains.

Hell Exploded is written in what could be called burlesque-stage oratory, and Campbell claims he told the guard at Tyler that "we had been brought up in the belief that eating was a necessity which should not be suspended longer than a few weeks at a time, and that we would consider it a mark of genuine thoughtfulness reminded if he would connect us with a few chunks of bread and a saw-log of sausage or a few wheelbarrowsful of tamales."

The guard, also an orator of sorts, responded sarcastically that "In the sweat of thy face shalt thou eat bread," before refusing to get them anything to eat.

Then, in winter weather, they were transferred to an exposed flat car and hauled, still unfed, to Rusk. There, from the train depot, they were marched the mile and a half to the penitentiary and processed inside.

Still not accepting the reality of prison, Campbell claims they were "robbed of their money and tobacco and what else we happened to have about us" by the guards. When he asked for his money back he was informed, "Hell is all you'll ever get back," and then was soundly cussed out.

After the hated neck shackles had been removed, the new inmates were measured by the Bertillion clerk and interviewed as to past personal histories, to which Campbell told him he was "in the habit of breaking into penitentiaries." The clerk, Campbell, recalls, simply "bit his chin in silence."

But Charles Campbell had just entered into what he later referred to as "that bifurcated hell of Texas": the Rusk penitentiary. Then, "robbed of their personal possessions," shaved, and showered, they were issued their striped prison uniforms. In his state of nakedness, Campbell put on the uniform, and for the first time the reality of his situation finally appears to have hit him.

At that point, he recalls in *Hell Exploded*, he suddenly felt totally humiliated. He admonishes the readers of *Hell Exploded*: "Young man, old man,—men! Don't go to that place! If Fate ever says you must go—*die first!* [narrator's italics]. Welcome death instead of worse than death."

Campbell and the other new prisoners then received their first meal in thirty-six hours, a typical Rusk prison meal consisting of cold corn bread and raw, fat bacon.

His second day in prison he was assigned to a work detail outside the walls of the prison and turned out with a wood squad that morning.

After being issued axes, he and three other inmates were harnessed to a wagon and forced to haul it to the woods, cut a cord of wood each, load the wagon, and then haul it back to the prison unit. That accomplished, they were then required to unload it and pitch the wood up tier after tier to a level of about forty feet. His hands, he recalled, were two large blisters at the end of his first day.

The next morning, in intense agony, he requested something to relieve the pain. After breakfast he reported to his field boss expecting to get something for the blisters and excruciating pain, only to find the guard had obtained "relief" in the form of a rusty crowbar and rough-handled pick. He was then reassigned to work the iron ore beds. On only his second day in prison, he had antagonized the guards controlling him, and this was his first dose of retaliatory prison guard humor.

In misery, he picked up the tools and reported to the field with his squad. Within ten minutes the blisters on both hands had broken and he had lost all skin on both palms. The handles of his crowbar and axe were stained red with his blood, he reports. In an act that suggests he still was not completely aware that he was in prison and working on a chain gang, he naively asked to be excused from work because of his hands.

The guard's response indicated that Campbell was not the only one with a sharp tongue and smart mouth: "Get the hell away from here, you G-d d—d ____ ____ ____ ____. What've I got to do with yer d—d hands? Git, G-d d—n ye, an' go to work!" was the answer.

Campbell recalled that, at that moment, he wanted to die. Wrapping his hands in rags, he made it through the day and spent the night rubbing a piece of stolen bacon fat into them to reduce the swelling.

After his initial indoctrination to prison life on the wood crew, he spent the next three months working on an ore drilling squad. He seems to have learned to control his thoughts and words on these work assignments because, based upon his "attitude adjustment," he was assigned to a roustabout squad cutting brush.

Not content to leave well enough alone, Campbell quickly created new problems for himself. While cutting a wasp-infested bush, Campbell found himself being repeatedly stung. The field boss, sitting on a horse nearby, was taking delight in watching Campbell's misery.

When the guard yelled at him to work faster, Campbell responded that he would continue chopping the bush if the officer would "first pull the fire out of their tails." The guard, with no sense of humor, leveled his rifle on Campbell and threatened to blow his brains out.

Campbell, whether out of fear or simple agitation, then chopped the bush in a manner that it fell on the officer and his horse, creating a distraction allowing Campbell to escape.

Immediately, he realized the idiocy of his action and proceeded on foot and alone back to the prison unit and turned himself in, expecting the prison officials there to understand his actions.

Instead, he was taken to an alley inside the walls of the penitentiary, held down by six inmate "building tenders," and administered lashes with a strap, which he described as a very thick and heavy piece of leather about three inches wide, two and one-half feet long, and fastened into a handle about a foot and one-half in length.

The strap Campbell described was a version of the hated bat, and despite Texas laws limiting the administration of a lashing to thirty-nine strokes and prohibiting the breaking of skin on the prisoner, Campbell claims he was given at least sixty lashes. His entire body, including buttocks and legs, he reported, was saturated in blood.

The physical damage was so bad, he claimed, that for the next two weeks he was forced to sleep on his stomach. Despite his pain and misery, he was reassigned the next day to his squad and forced to work. Later recalling the beating he had received, he proclaims, "I hold myself today as standing delivered from a hell to which merciful God would not condemn a man's soul."

This severe beating with the bat and his realization that he was lucky to have survived it, seem to mark a time in his sentence where he accepts his situation as a convict in the Texas prison system.

At this point in *Hell Exploded*, Charles Campbell really begins to vent his bitterness and hatred for that prison system. He recounts several instances of other inmates allegedly being needlessly tortured and even killed by merciless prison guards.

One story involves Henry Tumlin (Campbell misspells the last name), in which he presents a far different version than Tomlin himself. While Tomlin, in *Henry Tomlin, the man who fought the brutality and oppression of the ring in the state of Texas for eighteen years and won*, claims to have refused to work during sixteen years at Rusk, Campbell claims Tomlin was injured and couldn't work.

In many ways *Hell Exploded* parallels Tomlin's narrative. At times there almost seems to have been collaboration between the two former prisoners, however too many critical events vary in details, and at one point Campbell refers to Tumlin "...where he is today if death has not released him, long-haired, sunken-eyed and emaciated, languishing away in life in a prison dungeon far from the sight and knowledge of the world."

After his strapping for attempting to escape his work crew, Campbell was sent to a wood camp some ten miles from the main prison unit, probably the notorious Alto wood camp. Here he was removed from the confines of the state prison at Rusk and leased out to a private company where, he claims, the living and working conditions were even more wretched. And yet his warped sense of narrative continues as he describes the camp food:

> Here are a few diets which the boys were fond of saying would be preferable to prison fare: Stewed fish hooks, baked centipede, boiled baled hay, shredded underwear and fricasseed brick bats with linseed oil sauce.

As was very often common during this period in the Texas prison work camps, self-mutilation was rampant among the inmates assigned to the work details.

In an incident he swears was not of his own design, Campbell was involved in a logging accident in which another inmate chopped off the ends of three of Campbell's fingers. Claiming the guards suspected him of intentionally causing the accident as an excuse to go to the hospital and get out of work, he reported that he was forced to sit in the woods the remainder of the day in the hot sun without medicine or pain killer. The next day a huge iron weight was fastened around one of his legs, and he was placed in a train car and sent back to Rusk.

There, medical attention consisted of another inmate operating on his finger stubs: "Taking a lance he cut the stubs of fingers to the bone in three places. He then stripped back the skin and flesh like peeling a banana, and taking a clipper cut off the ends of the bones and lapped back the skin and sewed it like he was repairing a saddle."

After the inmate "doctor" had cauterized the fingers without the benefit of pain relievers, Campbell was thrown in the "luny's [sic] cell," chained to the wall by a steel ring, and left for two days without food, water, or medical treatment. On the third day he was given okra soup and water. He claims his hand and arm were swollen to twice their normal size as he hung from the chain.

Fearing gangrene would develop and he would completely lose his hand or arm, he found a piece of broken glass and sliced his hand to drain the blood and puss. After forty days in that "luny cell," he was sent to the pipe foundry to tender the coal furnaces.

There, he claims, he was locked into a five-by-eight-foot space in front of the furnaces and forced to shovel coal for twelve-hour shifts, without the benefit of water, in the roasting temperatures. Claiming he could spit on the rock walls and the spittle would "sputter like dropping water on a hot stove," he performed this work for two weeks. At the end of this assignment, he charges, his body looked like a cadaver and was almost a solid blister. Again, he alleges, he was denied any medical treatment.

Then he was sent back to the wood camp.

At this point the guards were so confrontational with him that he feared they were conspiring to give him work assignments he could not possibly complete to create an excuse to kill him out in the woods where there would be no witnesses.

Feeling he was about to be murdered, he ran again and in the process managed to successfully elude the bloodhounds and guards.

But for the second time he had a change of heart and again turned around and surrendered himself to the officials at the main prison unit. He was immediately returned to the wood crew, expecting a repeat of the strapping he had received after the first escape incident.

Instead, he returned to find that another officer had been placed in charge of the work crew. To his surprise, he was not punished and was also allowed to serve out his remaining time in relative peace with the prison guards and officials.

His newfound spirit of cooperation with prison officials took a completely out-of-character turn when Campbell actually credits the new work squad sergeant with motivating him to write *Hell Exploded* after his release from Rusk.

Campbell recalls, "…when I served out the last day of my time, and was preparing to leave, he called me inside his office and shook my hand and bade me God speed, and cautioned me to not think of returning for revenge—to write."

"I have not betrayed your trust," he writes of the unnamed guard, "I have not included you with those who tortured me." Despite the humane treatment from this guard, however, Campbell could never completely temper his bitter and angry narrative about the system that had incarcerated him at Rusk.

With regards to the prison guards who imprisoned him, he recorded:

> I intended to devote a chapter to the discussion of guards, but after a mature consideration I decided that I would not defile a clean sheet of paper in any such way. They are sixty degrees beneath the contempt of a worn-out, mangey [*sic*] circus monkey, and to

compliment them by calling them anything would be an honor which I will not confer.

Defiant to the very end, Charles C. Campbell fought the guards and the system that imprisoned him for a crime he admits he was guilty of committing.

That defiance is perhaps best illustrated in the final paragraph of *Hell Exploded*:

> I was born and raised in Texas, if I am ashamed to own it; am going to remain here because I am not afraid to, and those not liking my explosion can find me any day, when I will argue the matter with them verbally, on paper, in court, "in the neck," or any other old place.

Charles Campbell marched up to the gates of Rusk penitentiary that first day, sometime in the 1890s, with an obvious attitude problem and a tendency to let his sarcasm get him into almost continuous trouble with his prison guards.

Given the physical abuse he endured as a result of his words and actions, it is probably fortunate that he only served a two-year sentence in the place he regarded as *"Hell Exploded."*

Given the severe punishments he was subjected to and the continuing retaliation from the guards, had his sentence been longer in duration, hell would probably have buried him.

Chapter Twenty-Two

Where, in God's Name, Were the Prison Chaplains?

If conditions during the Texas convict lease system were as barbaric as the inmates claimed they were—and the 1910 Texas legislative *Report of the Investigating Committee* suggests they were—where were the ministers and priests serving as prison chaplains in the midst of this, and why weren't they speaking out?

The answer is that they were almost always assigned to the main units at Huntsville and Rusk and almost never allowed to visit the sawmill camps, railroad crews, and coal mines where the convicts were leased to private companies. Medical doctors, who were mandated by Texas law to visit the camps, were noticeably lax in their duties, and ministers were never required and often not allowed to visit the camps.

State law also stipulated that prison officials not require inmates to work on Sundays, but we know from almost every memoir of that period that during the growing season, inmates worked seven days a week in the fields.

But in the main units at Rusk and Huntsville and on some of the state-owned farm units, the Sabbath was at least marginally recognized as a day of rest.

Almost every annual report contains some mention of the chaplains and the status of their programs with the inmates. In addition to attending to the religious needs of the prisoners, the chaplains often were also responsible for teaching literacy classes, and the Texas prison system has offered inmate education programs continuously since the late 1800s.

Sometimes prisoners would assume religious duties and become "convict preachers." Famed gunslinger and convicted murderer John Wesley Hardin served as superintendent of Sunday school classes at the Huntsville unit in the 1890s.

Beecher Deason wrote of the Ferguson Farm, "For pastime on Sunday we went to church, played dominoes, checkers, and sometimes baseball,"[1] suggesting that at least occasionally religious services were available, even if conducted by an inmate preacher.

But while chaplains were kept away from the scenes of much of the mistreatment of convicts, they were by no means silently looking the other direction. One Huntsville chaplain in particular, the Reverend Jake Hodges, took on the prison administration in the early 1900s—with corporal punishment the impetus of his investigations and reports.

Since medical facilities were noticeably absent in the work camps, the worst cases of mistreatment that resulted in near-death or permanent crippling would be transferred back to either Huntsville or Rusk for treatment.

As these convicts would return to Huntsville, often with crippled or missing limbs and sometimes with backs completely raw and infected from strapping, Reverend Hodges would find a way to talk with them and record the details of their mistreatment in the labor camps.

He would then document his findings in the form of "official reports," which he would send to state officials, focusing primarily upon the penitentiary board members.

Prison administrators and state officials had become used to Hodge's accusations and generally credited them to his being too sympathetic to prisoners eager to exaggerate their cases. As a result, to his frustration, his reports were either publicly denied by prison officials or more often, simply ignored.

As his frustration grew, he looked for other avenues to educate the public on the conditions in the work camps. In 1908 he found a willing and capable ally in a young journalist with the *San Antonio Daily Express* named George Waverly Briggs.

At Hodges' urging, Briggs conducted a thorough investigation of the Texas prison system and published his findings in a five-week Sunday edition series from December 1908 through the first two weeks of 1909. The result was a public outcry over the conditions of the inmates being leased out of the prison system. As that public outrage grew in numbers and intensity, the issue finally became important enough that it forced the governor to request an official investigation by members of the legislature.

That investigation quickly led to the *Report of the Penitentiary Investigating Committee* issued in August 1910. In it, the committee stated unequivocally, "We recommend that the contract and labor share farm systems be abolished not later than January 1, 1912, and that all convicts be kept and worked in the prisons and upon the State farms...."[2]

The recommendations were adopted, and officially at least, the convict lease system ended in 1912. The prison system, however, to accommodate the large number of inmates it now found itself required to house and care for, began purchasing farmland—often from the companies who had previously hired the convicts from the state. In many ways, inmates alleged, Texas replaced the mistreatment of convicts by private enterprise with equal or even greater mistreatment by prison guards on the geographically isolated farm units that were created.

But one of the most shameful episodes in post-slavery Texas came to an official end in 1912. Many factors came into play in bringing about the abolishment of the convict lease system, but the dogged determination and persistence of the Reverend Jake Hodges played the greatest role.

During the publication of Briggs' investigative series from December 1908 through January 1909, Hodges was fired by the prison system—terminated from his job as a chaplain—but his insistence that terrible injustice was taking place in Texas penitentiaries led to the eventual abolition of the system he abhorred.

---

1   Deason, Beecher, *Seven Years in Texas Prisons*, pg. 7.

2   *Report of the Penitentiary Investigating Committee including All Exhibits and Testimony Taken by the Committee, Published by Order of the House of Representatives, August 1910*, pg. 16.

Chapter Twenty-Three

Lookout, Dawg Boy!

The bloodhounds used by the Texas prison system have been considered possibly the best in the world for *at least* a century. Some of the bloodlines run back nearly that far. Texas prison bloodhounds are not just used in tracking escaped inmates, their services are requested by the FBI, DEA, state law enforcement agencies inside and outside Texas, and by search and rescue squads throughout America.

During a recent high-profile prison escape, a newscaster referred to the fact that Texas prison dogs, accompanied by inmate kennel men, had been dispatched to assist in the search.

The expression "inmate kennel men" probably brought chuckles to a few older guards and even a few ex-convicts who might have watched the newscast. That particular term did not exist until recently, after the reorganization of the "new" Texas Department of Criminal Justice. The "old" Texas Department of Corrections, or TDC, was far less complimentary in the classification of inmates who handled the bloodhounds.

A decade ago the inmates who handled the dogs in the field were simply known as "dog boys." Even earlier, convicts working in the lease camps during the 1800s probably wouldn't have known how to respond to the expression "inmate kennel men." But inmates did handle the dogs back then, only they were known commonly as dawg boys.

Concern about bloodhounds and the respect for their ability to track is recorded in the earliest of the narratives. After his successful escape from a lease farm near the Sabine River in the 1880s, John Dunn realized the dogs would soon be on his trail.

"I had heard of an old trick from a fellow trail-driver," he recalled, "and I was willing to risk it now. I gathered every can of pepper they [a rural family] had in the cupboard. Then I started out again. I scattered more than three cans of pepper on my back trail. I don't know what happened when the hounds stuck their noses to that—but I have a pretty good idea. At the time my only hope was that they would be turned into sneezing, mixed-up wrecks."[1]

There is no record indicating his pepper tactic worked (the trainers claim it won't), but Dunn did escape, never to be recaptured and returned to Texas.

Charles Campbell, describing his escape in *Hell Exploded*, recorded he could immediately hear the yelping of the dogs on his trail.

"As soon as they hear the report of a gun they become furious," he wrote. "The biped dogs [guards] keep the quadruped ones necked in twos, and when a shot is heard they unneck the last named dogs and away they go like the wind; that is, if the wind gets up and flies."[2]

Campbell also wrote of the futility of trying to elude the bloodhounds: "They will go, or sail, to the spots straight as a bee line, and a thousand to one they will tree the man before he goes two miles. They are thoroughly trained from pups to run men, and it is next to an impossibility to beat them, considering the almost invariable excitement of those trying to escape."[3]

Also in the 1890s, Charles Favor recalled, "The state keeps bloodhounds, at all times, at a convenient point; and in the event a convict escapes, they are put on the culprit's trail. It is very difficult to elude the dogs, and should they catch a convict their viciousness is extreme. With each pack of dogs is kept a trusty, whose duty it is to care for the dogs, which consists in feeding, watering and keeping them clean. They are kept in kennels at night and are locked in. In the morning the dog-trusty gets out the dogs and keeps them stationed at such a place, that he may be ready in case an attempt to escape is made."[4]

Beecher Deason, in 1928, escaped the Clemens Farm in Brazoria County on the Texas Gulf Coast. In an effort to throw off the bloodhounds, he ran in a zigzag course, climbed up and down several trees, backtracked, and circled before climbing into a tall tree. He recalled later, "Pretty soon I heard the dogs on my trail."[5]

Deason also recalled the guards had a habit of letting the dogs chew an escaped prisoner when they caught him. On that occasion he eluded the guards but he didn't elude the dogs: "The next time they bayed, they bayed at the tree I was in. One old dog kept circling around and around the tree in widening circles. But the rest of them were letting it out at the foot of the tree. Two big black fellows kept rearing up the tree, looking up at me as if to say, 'You are our meat.'"[6]

The guards soon rode up but instead of following the signals of the dogs, the mounted field bosses argued about which way Deason had run and never bothered to look up in the tree. They herded the dogs away, and when the hounds tried to backtrack to the same spot, the guards called the search off that day.

Deason escaped that day only to be recaptured later.

For obvious reasons, strong bonds develop between these intelligent, loyal dogs and the men who train and care for them. The value of bloodhounds was shown in an alleged incident during the 1920s:

In a chilling account, Mrs. J.E. King, chairwoman of the prison advisory board, testified before a 1925 prison investigating committee in Austin. Although she reported several suspicious inmate deaths, one in particular shocked the legislative committee and led to statewide newspaper editorials calling for a massive change in the Texas prison system.

In 1925 the convict lease system had been "officially" dead for thirteen years, however Texas had replaced the lease system by purchasing much of the land the camps had been located on and simply running the farm units with prison guards instead of lessees.

Assigned to one of those former lease camps was an inmate by the name of Fred Chance. On February 11, 1925, Mrs. King testified that inmate Chance had written her a letter warning that guards were about to kill him. The transcript of her testimony gives the details:

> The gruesome death of Frank Chance, a native of Chile, who was shot to death by guards on one of the prison farms, as related by Mrs. King, set the committee members aghast. It was charged Chance had been compelled to dig his own grave. Mrs. King declared the man was murdered in cold blood, and that she had tried in vain to obtain the discharge of one of the guards, F.E. Hamilton, who was charged with complicity in the case.
>
> Mrs. King received a letter from Chance asking her to come to the prison to save him, because he feared he was to be killed. According to the letter, the guards had taken Chance out in a field where they made him dig a hole, which he inferred was to be his grave.
>
> "They asked me how tall I was," said Chance's letter, which Mrs. King read. "When I told them six feet,

they ordered me to dig a hole six feet long, as that was to be my grave."

Mrs. King hastened to the prison farm as soon as she could, but was delayed several days.

"When I arrived, Chance was dead," continued the witness. "He had been shot to death by the guards. His death was a cold-blooded, brutal murder."[7]

What was the reasoning for killing the inmate?

According to Mrs. King, "The guards explained they had shot him because he had threatened to kill a dog, and they thought it their duty to protect state property by killing the prisoner."

The bloodhounds used by the Texas prison system have been considered possibly the best in the world for over a hundred years. It is impossible to place a value on their use.

But in 1925 a prison bloodhound was evidently worth more than the life of inmate Fred Chance.

1   Evans, Max, *Long John Dunn of Taos, From Texas Outlaw to New Mexico Hero*, pg. 50.
2   Campbell, Charles C., *Hell Exploded.*, pg. 28.
3   Ibid.
4   Favor, Charles A., *Twenty-Two Months in the Texas Penitentiary*, pg. 67.
5   Deason, Beecher, *Seven Years in Texas Prisons*, pg. 16.
6   Ibid.
7   "Mother King Tells of Prison Killings," *Houston Post-Dispatch*, February 11, 1925, front page.

Chapter Twenty-Four

(1921-1928)

Seven Years in Texas Prisons

The Texas Prison Memoir of Beecher Deason

One of the boys still had a little life in him, and he tried to raise up. When he did, the least one of the building tenders hit him with a billy or club and knocked him back to the floor. Then the boy they had beaten was made to go down there where the boys had bled and wash up the blood. While he did that the building tender—the one who had done the stabbing—walked up and down the aisle, raving like a maniac. He licked the blood off his knife and asked us if any of the rest of us wanted to.

Beecher Deason was sentenced to prison in Texas in the early 1920s and reported to Huntsville shortly after the legislature had abolished the convict lease system. What he found was a prison system that had purchased many of the former lease camps and converted them into prison work farms.

Deason, like many other inmates, found the terrible conditions on these camps and farms had changed little since the days when private companies had "leased" inmate labor in Texas for often less than a dollar a day.

Deason would later write an account of his experience titled *Seven Years in Texas Prisons*. Clearly indicating he felt conditions had not improved since the convict lease years, he asks questions of the reader: "Did you ever see the Devil? Have you ever been in Hell? Did you ever have an angel pay a visit to your cell in solitary confinement where men are seldom fed?"

These questions and others of likewise sordid nature are asked and answered in *Seven Years in Texas Prisons*. "I've seen it all in reality in the land of the living dead," he concludes in this narrative of his confinement in the Texas prison system.

Although Deason is vague regarding the events leading up to his conviction and imprisonment, especially with regards to dates, *Seven Years in Texas Prisons* suggests in various passages that the time frame is 1921 through 1928, and that he served on several different Texas prison work farms throughout the system during that period.

Deason served five different prison sentences between the ages of seventeen and thirty-one. One of those sentences was served in Arkansas, which he claimed was an even more brutal experience than the Texas system. Most of his prison incarceration, however, was spent in Texas.

He was a petty criminal serving time for burglary, theft, forgery, and bootlegging. He was also somewhat unusual in that he freely admitted guilt for the charges that led to each of his convictions.

His experience behind prison bars began at Huntsville when he was still a teenager. That first night inside the brick walls of the prison headquarters unit in Huntsville, he was locked in a cell as the only occupant. Sitting on his crude bunk, staring out among the cages of other "doomed" men, he found himself imprisoned with only his thoughts and fears.

And he was terrified.

Criminologists and psychologists have never succeeded in discovering a method or approach that effectively prevents a young person from becoming a criminal. But Beecher Deason identifies that moment when he could have been turned away from his criminal lifestyle: It was that first night sitting inside a cell surrounded by steel bars.

"I want you to know that my feelings reached the depths of despair," he later recalled. "That, I think, was or would have been the psychological time to have pardoned me."

But he was convicted and sentenced to prison; his moment for changing his ways had slipped away. But that first experience and impression inside the Huntsville unit remained with him the rest of his life. "Anyway I didn't die or get killed that night...," he later wrote.

If his first impression terrified him that night, his actual prison experience, beginning the next morning, would signal only more misery and fear.

He was initially assigned to shovel coal in the "dummy," or lower yard, of the prison. Later he was assigned to a work crew that traveled outside the prison daily and worked in the wood camps scattered throughout the piney woods around Huntsville. On his wood crew, he was expected to chop a cord of wood each day. This quota of wood was excessive, but many of the earlier lease camps had required more. Outside the prison walls, however, Deason discovered that his one cord per day was required regardless of the weather or whether he was sick or injured.

Conditions on the work crew were as bad as anything he might have imagined prior to coming to prison. Not only were working conditions brutal and unsafe, the inmates were fed very little food, and those rations they received in the field were almost inedible.

After a month his work crew mutinied over the bad food. Since he was still a new inmate, he initially refused to join the work stoppage out of fear of punishment by the guards, and he was, in fact, spared being sent to the "hole" or solitary confinement with the rest of his squad. Immediately, however, some of the older veteran inmates took him aside and explained the "inmate code" to him.

He would be branded a snitch, they threatened him, if he didn't join his crew in lockup. To emphasize their point, they threatened to beat him on the spot if he didn't go to the warden and demand to join the work stoppage.

Wisely, he had a change of mind, and the warden did send him to solitary confinement briefly but spared him a beating. The inmate squad leader who had instigated the stoppage was later administered the strap.

Early in his prison career, this incident made clear to Deason the harsh reality and difficulty of trying to survive in the penitentiary. Deason was a petty criminal in prison for doing nonviolent crimes on the outside. Inside prison, however, he quickly learned that refusing to join his fellow convicts in these situations could lead to his death.

After his release from solitary confinement, he was assigned a job helping set up a shingle mill inside the main prison unit. Given his prior background working in East Texas sawmills, this was a relatively easy job assignment—especially compared to his brief experience on the crew chopping cords of wood.

The inmate he was working with, however, fabricated a story that Deason had tried to push him into a saw blade, and as a result he was reassigned. This time he found himself shipped out to one of the farm units.

Again he was paired with another inmate and given a job assignment. This time his work partner was an old Negro convict named Edd, who taught him the age-old convict trick of "slow bucking" on the job:

"...White boy, you listen to this old nigger and you will get by easy." I asked him what he meant. He said, "You watch me when dat boss man comes ova here and ask me to do sumpin." Pretty soon the guard did come over and called Edd. Old Edd pretended not to hear him. The guard called him a second time in a louder voice. Old Edd raised up quickly, jerked off his hat and shouted, "Oh, good gracious alive, Oh laudy, sah," and looked like he was scared to death. The guard just laughed and said, "You better go to work, you old black devil." Then old Edd said, "Yassah, cap'n, you know I will, sah." After the guard left, old Edd told me "Now see, white boy, you just do like dat, and you will get along all right."

Deason's reaction was to laugh and dismiss old Edd's advice, but what he didn't realize that day was that the old convict had given him some information that would later save him from a strapping and the dreaded "hole."

One day (and he gives no specific date) the guards summoned him and attached a neck chain to him. He and several other prisoners were then shackled together and transferred to the nearby Ferguson Farm on a mule-drawn wagon.

Like his first experience outside Huntsville on the wood crew, he found the Ferguson Farm to be much more primitive and the living and working conditions far more brutal and dangerous.

The Ferguson Farm was one of the relatively new state owned prison farms that had replaced the convict lease camps after 1912. It was located far enough from Huntsville to be isolated from the public's scrutiny and had already developed a reputation among inmates as a brutal and sadistic place to be assigned.

Seven Years in Texas Prisons gives one of the earliest known descriptions of what the Ferguson Farm looked like in the 1920s. "At first appearance it looked like a large dairy farm," Deason writes. "The loft of the building was similar to those seen in small churches. The building proper was about 120 feet long, with a hall in the center, but instead of walls in the hall there were bars and we called it the picket. A guard was stationed in the picket constantly."

Deason found the farm to be as brutal as the inmate rumors had suggested. Discipline was far more severe at Ferguson and included a variety of punishment tools, which he referred to as "implements of torture."

Deason describes the carpenter's horse upon which inmates were forced to sit for hours, unable to touch the floor with their feet. Another common punishment was the use of chains to suspend an inmate. Other times, the barrel was used in which inmates were forced to stand on top of the wooden kegs until their legs cramped.

Building tenders, or inmates serving as guards over the other prisoners, existed throughout the Texas prison system when Deason was serving time. He would have had contact with them at Huntsville, but it is at Ferguson that he details the violent behavior of these privileged convicts.

The tenders were usually those inmates who were biggest, toughest, and most violent. Because of them, only a small number of salaried prison guards would be required to supervise a building or even the entire farm, since the actual control and discipline of the prisoners was usually handled by these building tenders.

They, in return, were allowed special privileges such as single cells, better food, freedom of movement around the unit, and the right to extort other inmates for favors.

Reports of the use of building tenders can be found in prison narratives as early as the 1870s, and these inmate guards would be utilized by the Texas prison system until the 1980s when they were abolished only after extensive litigation by the federal judicial system in class-action lawsuits against the state.

But in the 1920s they were legal and used throughout the system. At Ferguson, Deason writes, "They carried dirk knives and clubs similar to a policeman's billy and believe me they would certainly use them if the occasion arose."

"I have seen them make all the men, except a chosen few, get on their bunks and stay there during a rainy day when we couldn't work. If you wanted to get off of your bunk for anything," he continues, "you had to get permission from the tender."

He describes, in graphic detail, a later incident at the Eastham Farm, giving the first date in the booklet, 1922, when he witnessed a building tender kill two inmates with a home-made knife and nearly beat a third prisoner to death. After the assault, the building tender walked among the inmates on their bunks, licking the blood off the knife, and asking if anybody else "wanted some."

He also recorded, in 1925, that another building tender killed an inmate in the dining area without provocation and without any repercussions from the prison officials.

Since the Ferguson unit was an agricultural farm, most of the inmates assigned there were required to do field work. The extensive fields at Ferguson were divided into blocks of about thirty acres each, separated by a narrow road called a "turn row" that led from the main prison unit out to the crops. The convict workers were organized into hoe squads and sent out each morning along the turn rows to a predetermined spot. The inmates would then be ordered to "catch a row" and start working down it—chopping grass or aerating the soil—in a procedure basically unchanged on Texas prison farm units today.

On Deason's second day in the field, he and his squad received an "orientation" from the field boss on horseback:

> I'm going to tell you what I expect of you and what you can expect of me. You all know that I didn't send you here…Boys, you are all here because you were convicted of a crime against society. You are going to wear my clothes, eat my grub, sleep in my building and you are going to work! I've got some cotton and you men have some grass in my cotton and I want it out! You hear me?

The field captain then ordered them to all remove their hats in his presence, something that was particularly galling to Deason for some reason, and he ignored the order—the only man in his squad not to jerk the cap off immediately. Instead, he looked away trying to decide what to do.

This undated photograph shows Captain Hickman supervising the transporting of cotton bales by an inmate on an unnamed Brazoria County prison farm.
Photo source: Brazoria County Historical Museum Photograph Collection

"Old Bully, take that hat off before I knock it off," the captain threatened him. When Deason continued to ignore him, the officer started to run him down with his horse. At the movement of the horse, Deason snatched his hat from his head and shouted, "Oh good gracious alive, sir," and explained that he was hard of hearing. When the captain started after him again, Deason jumped around, hat in hand, yelling "Oh Laudy, sah, good gracious alive, Cap'n, you know I am." Finally the captain started laughing, and Deason had worked his way out of a tight place.

The trick that old Edd had taught him earlier, when he was still new to the prison system, had saved him from a strapping and a period in the "hole."

Deason and the other convicts worked the fields six days a week. On Saturdays, he recalled, they would sometimes come in a half hour early so they could bathe and change clothes. If the hoe squads had shown good progress during the week, tobacco would sometimes be issued on Saturday evenings.

Except during harvest season, Sunday would be the only day of rest. Ferguson inmates in the 1920s typically, according to Deason, spent the day off playing board games in the dormitories or in good weather, organizing occasional baseball games. Church services were available but were usually conducted by inmate preachers and were not well attended.

Deason uses *Seven Years in Texas Prisons* as a warning to any young readers who might be considering a life of crime. In one direct and very clear passage, he writes of the negative effects the older convicts had on younger inmates.

Counseling young readers, he admonishes, "But the bad element rules. A person has got to pretend he is one of the boys, that he is just as bad as any of them. If he doesn't do that, if he tries to act like a man and hold up for what is right and looks askance at things they do, they will make life so miserable for him that it will be unbearable."

This was a lesson he had himself learned the hard way when he had refused early in his sentence to join his work squad when they had "bucked."

He also describes in effective detail the humiliation and anguish he felt at the constant verbal abuse from the guards: "It has the effect of making you self-conscious, timid, and gives you a feeling of inferiority, and it is hard to get away from—mighty hard."

Deason eventually made trusty and almost immediately rewarded the state's trust in him by escaping on a mule and then swimming the Trinity River. Stealing a shotgun and some clothes from a nearby house, he panicked when he heard dogs barking and thought the prison bloodhounds were on his trail. Exhausted and dehydrated, he stopped at another house and stole some food and water but was turned in by a farmer who had witnessed him from a field. Incredibly, he was not punished after his recapture.

He escaped a second time, from the Clemons (officially, "Clemens") Farm on the Brazos River, in Brazoria County, in 1928. This time he avoided the tracking dogs but spent so much time and energy avoiding the hounds and guards that, exhausted, he eventually asked a farmer to call the prison officials to come and get him. Again he was not beaten for escaping, but this time he did lose all his "good time credits" toward early parole.

Deason describes several mass escapes from Texas prison units in the 1920s, including one involving seventeen inmates at Eastham Camp #2, but he does not give a specific date.

The events in *Seven Years in Texas Prisons* are not presented in any chronological order. Toward the end of his narrative, he mentions another personal escape attempt, this time from the Blueridge Farm in November of 1925. Climbing through the roof of the barracks during a midday rainstorm, he followed a drainage ditch until it widened and then rode a

This very old photograph shows inmates loading cane on the Masterson Plantation at Otey. The plantation is now known as the Ramsey unit and Otey is today a small community of prison employees located outside Rosharon, in Brazoria County. Photo source: Brazoria County Historical Museum Photograph Collection

This early 1900s photograph shows the sugarcane mill at the Clemens State Farm in southern Brazoria County. Photo source: Brazoria County Historical Museum Photograph Collection

floating gate post about three miles downstream until darkness set in.

Wet and freezing, he approached an oilrig to steal dry clothes and food but was caught by the workers and turned

The infamous Eastham Prison Farm. This early but undated photo shows the main building of what has historically been the most dreaded and notorious prison in Texas. Photo courtesy of Robert H. Russell and the Texas Prison Museum, Huntsville, Texas.

over to the police. Taken to Houston, he was jailed until his captain could retrieve him once more.

For the third time in his narrative, he claims he was not punished for attempting to escape. Escapes and escape attempts have always been dealt with harshly by prison officials, but in the 1920s many attempts resulted in the inmate being shot. State law and prison policy justified this as necessary to deter the attempts. That Deason would have made three attempts with no punitive reaction from the guards or prison officials is impossible to explain.

Beecher Deason eventually did break his personal cycle of discharging and returning to Texas prisons. He credits his rehabilitation to meeting and marrying "a good woman."

But his successful transition from criminal to law-abiding citizen was not without difficulties. In *Seven Years in Texas Prisons*, he describes the problems of surviving in society while carrying the stigma of being an ex-convict.

For a man who served time on some very tough prison farms during very turbulent years, he is surprisingly candid and positive in his assessment of the role of police officers in our society.

The idea of ex-offenders being hounded by the law is dismissed outright. "If a burglary is committed it is the most natural thing for him [the policeman] to check on all known burglars," he writes. "A good many people teach their children to be afraid of an officer and that is wrong, they should teach them to love and respect an officer of any kind; to look on them as their friend and protector."

Revealing that he himself had been the primary suspect when burglaries had happened in his town after his release from prison, he states, "I didn't blame the officers. I took it as part of the price I had to pay for trying to beat the law in my younger days."

The lack of anger or vindictiveness in his words, combined with the objective and evenhanded approach he took to counseling young readers about the criminal lifestyle, suggests that Beecher Deason may well have rehabilitated himself while in prison. On the other hand, he doesn't appear to have been subjected to the degree of brutality that writers of other narratives suffered.

Unlike many of the narratives from 1875 to 1925, Deason takes a more conciliatory approach in his prison memoirs and claims to have written his narrative with an honest desire to "keep many boys and young men from following in my footsteps."

Chapter Twenty-Five

That First Night in the Pen

Society has debated for centuries as to whether or not prison serves as a deterrent to crime. For some criminals who serve sentence after sentence, the answer is obviously "no."

Society also experiments with the "threat of prison" as a tool to straighten out wayward youngsters. In the 1980s a program called "Scared Straight" forced youth-at-risk to visit prisons and be "indoctrinated" by hard-core felons in an attempt to dissuade them from continuing their own criminal behavior. The results were disappointing.

Conditions in Texas prisons from the 1800s through the period of the Great Depression were known to be particularly harsh, even by the standards of the American South. So why then did some of these criminals continue their lifestyles until they achieved the obvious consequence: incarceration in a brutal prison system? The answer is that nobody really knows why, but it is obvious that the threat of imprisonment does not discourage criminal activities in many individuals.

And that answer is painfully obvious when today, one hundred years after some of these convict memoirs, Texas has over 125 prison units instead of just two.

But the consequences of advancing from being a petty criminal to a convicted felon are staggering, even to a youth bent upon a life of criminal behavior. The writings of these early convicts indicate most did not ever really stop to consider the consequences of their criminal actions.

And their recollections of their first night in the penitentiary also indicate they were terrified.

Beecher Deason, who entered the Huntsville unit in 1921, recalled that his first night locked with dangerous and desperate criminals was one in which he was filled with terror:

> I believe there is a time in nearly every criminal's life when he is terrified or so full of remorse that he would reform from crime if he were given a pardon. I think that time for me was on my first night in prison …I was assigned to a cell alone and, friends, as I sat there in that cell alone and listened to the grating clang of steel doors and the shuffling, restless movements of doomed men and the many other mysterious night noises of the big prison, I want you to know that my feelings reached the depths of despair…Anyway I didn't die or get killed that night….[1]

Much earlier, in 1885, Andrew George had also experienced that same despair and remorse and questioned how he had allowed himself to become a prison convict:

> In the evening of the first day I was taken to my cell and when I was alone I looked at my stripes and then at the iron bars and asked myself is this A.L. George, if so, how came him in such a place as this, and how long has he got to stay here—is this the kind of man his mother died praying for him to make?[2]

At the close of the 1800s, most Texas county courts operated on a two-term docket, usually a trial calendar in the spring and another in the fall, resulting in those accused and unable to post bond spending considerable time in county jail before their hearings. By many accounts some of these county jails operated in even worse conditions than the state prison units, and the first night in prison may not have necessarily been the worst experience in their criminal lives.

John Shotwell, whose extremely bitter narrative gives no positive credit to the Texas prisons from 1895 to 1909, suggests that his moment of despair occurred after his sentencing at the Mount Pleasant jail. Like Andrew George, he recalls the impact his conviction had on his mother:

> When the verdict of the jury was read my humiliation and embarrassment were great indeed, and for a few moments I could not speak. My fond and loving mother, while pleading for her accused boy, gave forth a pathetic sob which melted those present to tears, and touched every heart with tenderness and mercy. It was at this stage of life that I first realized the true value of a precious mother. In all the universe of God there is nothing more beautiful than a mother's love for her wayward son, and through all the changing scenes of life, in sunshine and in shadow, she is unchanged and unchangeable, and with silvery tresses and tottering form, she will follow him to the gutter, to the jail, to the asylum, to state prison or to the gallows, and her loving arms will encircle him, showing that her affection never falters nor wavers.
>
> The father may disinherit his son and drive him from the parental roof; the wife may abandon the man whom she promised to follow through failure and fortune; friend may forget or learn to despise friend, but a mother will follow her prodigal boy, begging and praying on her bended knees that he may make a better man.[3]

Bill Mills, who would serve seven separate prison sentences before giving up his criminal lifestyle, also recalled that terrible realization during his first night in a prison dorm on the Burleson and John Farm in 1910:

> Going back to my first night in prison, they assigned me to a bunk in the extreme end of the building. I was told by the other prisoners, and it was a fact, that a prisoner had been whipped so severely that he had died in the same bunk a short time before, so I didn't sleep too soundly on my shuck bed with those thoughts in my mind. When it was necessary for a prisoner to get out of his bed at night, he was required to shout "alley!" and the guard or tender would say "Go on."[4]

Milt Good, whose prison sentence began in 1925 after much of the barbaric conditions in the work camps had disappeared, also recalled the impact of that first night at Huntsville:

> No convict can ever forget his feelings when he hears those three large steel gates or doors clang behind him. His heart sinks and a feeling of hopelessness and helplessness seems to overwhelm him. I remember how I felt and others have told me they had the same sensations.[5]

J.S. Calvin, who did do "hard labor" after arriving at Rusk in 1898, writes of a first night of misery in the prison:

> ...four of us were conducted to a small cell where we were to spend the rest of the night. Our bedding consisted of a quilt to be spread on a concrete floor, without any pillow. As those large stone buildings were naturally cool, and as the evening's rain had made the

night uncomfortably cool, you can imagine about how we fared the rest of the night. In about two or three hours the gong sounded for the prisoners to get up and dress for breakfast though it seemed to me that it had been almost an age since we entered that cold cell, but we did not go to breakfast when the rest of the prisoners went, but remained in our cells until the other prisoners had got their breakfast and been assigned to their work for the day. [6]

Charles A. Favor, who had entered Rusk six years earlier in 1892, recalled the unsettling experience of spending that first night in the pen:

I sat down upon the run-a-round, little caring what should become of me. Tired and sleepy, and no place to lie! Sad and cheerless, and no one to comfort me. I thought of home and loved ones; of past associations, comforts and pleasures; and then rounding up in my dejected present I could not dispel the blackened cloud which hovered so closely about me. Then the "building tender" showed me a bed where I should sleep. It was on the bottom tier. I bunked with another man. His clothing was damp with perspiration; he had an odor about him that was not pleasant; the bed smelled from want of air, but I crowded in, and, notwithstanding the hardness of my bed, I fell asleep. How long I slept I do not know, but when I awakened I had not rested. [7]

Andrew Walker, in 1883, recalls his first night as so terrible that he honestly believed he had mistakenly been assigned to a lunatic asylum:

...I could not sleep and I suppose it was about 11 o'clock when all at once someone in the cell adjoining

Undated photograph showing two-tiered bunks on one of the state prison farm units. Photo source: Texas State Archives

ours commenced yelling at the top of his voice, and in a twinkling another one commenced, and still another and so on until there was a chorus of the most unearthly yells mingled with oaths and moaning that a person could imagine he were being ushered into Hades. The noise awoke my companions and one of them, an Irishman, grabbed hold of me and said for God's sake wake up Andy they have sure made a mistake and brought us to a lunatic asylum instead of a state prison.[8]

Walker, like the others, learned that first night that they were in for an extended period of "hell in a Texas pen." He, like each of the others, also adapted and survived his prison experience to eventually discharge and write about his memories and experiences as a Texas convict.

Society may never know for certain if the trauma of that first night in the penitentiary ever leads individuals to give up their lives of crime, but in each of these narratives it is painfully evident that the threat of prison before that first night did not deter the men in the beginning.

1 Deason, Beecher, *Seven Years in Texas Prisons*, pp. 1-2.
2 George, Andrew L., *The Texas Convict: Sketches of the Penitentiary, Convict Farms and Railroads, Together with Poems*, pp. 12-13.
3 Shotwell, John, *A Victim of Revenge or Fourteen Years in Hell*, pg. 9.
4 Mills, Bill, *25 Years Behind Prison Bars*, pg. 10.
5 Good, Milt (as told to W.E. Lockhart), *Twelve Years in a Texas Prison*, pp. 23-24.
6 Calvin, J.S., *Buried alive, or, A term in the Texas State Prison, 1898-1902: a chapter from real life*, pg. 30.
7 Favor, Charles A., *Twenty-Two Months in the Texas Penitentiary*, pp. 29-30.
8 Hennessy, T.D., *The life of A.J. Walker, an innocent convict: romantic, reads like fiction: real true life...*, pg. 45.

Chapter Twenty-Six

(1883-1902)

The Life of A.J. Walker, an Innocent Convict

The Texas Prison Memoir of Andrew J. Walker

In 1885 my cell mate was a young man serving a life sentence; like myself he was married and had one child. He and his wife were both born and reared in Texas. He wished to gain his liberty and seemed determined to do something that would enable him to secure freedom. One day he proposed to me that we each place both our hands on the saw and cut them off as we would be sure to get a pardon then. I told him I would rather put my neck there and cut my head off rather than my hands. Two weeks later he placed his right hand in a machine and cut off three fingers. One year later he was pardoned and I do believe that he was the proudest man on earth. After his arrival at home I received a letter from him and his wife telling me how happy they both were at being permitted to be together once more here on earth and that they hoped I would receive the same privilege in the near future.

On April 9, 1883, another new group of inmates arrived at Huntsville to begin their prison sentences. And as was usually the case with new arrivals, at least one of them was loudly protesting his innocence of the charges against him. This day that one particular inmate was especially vocal in proclaiming his innocence and the injustice of his imprisonment.

There is a good chance prison officials were already aware of the circumstances behind his murder conviction. The inmate was Andrew J. Walker, a well-known Confederate veteran, and his murder trials and conviction had captivated Texas newspapers for the previous nine years.

During those nine years Walker had been confined in the Galveston County jail while appealing his murder conviction. Walker was so adamant in his claims of innocence that twice during that period he escaped the jail only to voluntarily return for his next retrial dates.

During that period he was sentenced on two occasions to be hung. On one of those appeals, his stay was granted so near his execution date that he had already been measured for his own coffin.

Walker's original trial, and the subsequent appeals, was represented on both sides of the case by some of the most famous and successful legal talent in post-Civil War Texas. His appeals, involving most of that nine-year period, were pursued through the Texas court system to the state supreme court. The events were prominently covered by Texas newspapers but had also received extensive coverage outside the state.

The courtroom trial had been so emotional and the defense and prosecution so intense, that several defense witnesses were killed prior to or during the trial. Two of those killed were assassinated while asleep in their homes. During the subsequent trial of Walker's alleged accomplice, that codefendant was testifying on his own behalf when he was shot at while occupying the witness chair in the courtroom.

The *Galveston Daily News* later reported nearly $100,000 had been spent prosecuting and defending Walker's case—an astronomical sum in the 1872.

Although Walker was never able to get his murder conviction overturned, he did succeed in having his sentence reduced to life imprisonment, and on April 9, 1883, he was transferred from the Galveston County jail to the prison at Huntsville. Including his county jail time, he would eventually spend twenty-nine years of his life in a locked cell.

In 1883 a convicted man in Texas had few avenues in which to pursue his claims of innocence after he had been convicted. Once the trial appeals were exhausted, the inmate could only continue to publicly proclaim his innocence while hoping new evidence or testimony would clear him. Prison officials and fellow inmates have never been good listeners under those circumstances.

Occasionally a rare confession would result in the release of a falsely convicted inmate in prison. Two years after Walker arrived at Huntsville, another prisoner would also arrive proclaiming his innocence, and that inmate would eventually have a deathbed confession earn him an unconditional pardon and release from prison. The other inmate was Andrew L. George, who would later publish his memoir as *The Texas Convict*.

However, for Andrew J. Walker in 1883, there were no deathbed confessions to be deposed. Many of the witnesses, after all, were already dead—several killed before being able to testify.

So Walker adopted a novel approach to keeping his claims of innocence before the public in Texas: He hired a biographer and researcher named T.D. Hennessy. As a result, Walker's prison narrative is unique in that much of it was written *while* he was in prison.

Although the final publication is undated, it probably was released around 1903, the year after Walker finally was released from Huntsville. Titled *The Life of A.J. Walker, an innocent convict*, Walker's narrative describes his legal problems and imprisonment in Texas during the 1880s and 1890s.

Much of the book concentrates on the events leading up to Walker's transfer to the Huntsville unit.

One evening in May of 1872, a well-known citizen of Galveston County named Green Butler was assassinated on his ranch on Clear Creek. Immediately, two suspects were named, and one of them, Andrew J. Walker, surrendered to the sheriff on May 23. The other suspect, Jeff Black, also later surrendered.

Since Walker was also a well-known Galveston County citizen, the resulting trial became one of the most tumultuous and expensive murder prosecutions in that county's long and colorful history. In 1872 Galveston County and Texas were caught up in the political and social turmoil brought on by Reconstruction. Walker was a Confederate veteran, and this status seems to have been a factor in the notoriety of his trial and conviction, although he does not explain why or how.

As *The Life of A.J. Walker, an innocent convict* repeatedly points out, Walker was convicted on circumstantial evidence, with no motive for the murder ever established in the courtroom. The only witness to Butler's murder was a young Negro boy, who testified the killer drew his gun with his left hand and fired the deadly shots left-handed.

This statement became the focal point of Walker's defense. Witness after witness was called to the stand in court, and each testified that A.J. Walker was right-handed, but in the end their testimonies did not exonerate him.

The legal maneuvering in Walker's case is not all that make *The Life of A.J. Walker, an innocent convict* an unusual narrative. Hennessy recorded Walker's words and prison experiences during regular visits and interviews at the Huntsville prison during the 1880s.

Another fact that makes *The Life of A.J. Walker, an innocent convict* unique is that with the exception of John Wesley Hardin's autobiography, Walker's words give us one of the earliest descriptions of prison life in Texas.

Walker seems to have been a model inmate in prison and appears to have gained the respect and admiration of prison officials, many of whom would eventually petition for his pardon.

But on April 9, 1883, a protesting Andrew J. Walker entered prison at Huntsville considered by many lucky to have escaped the hangman's noose on two separate occasions.

He arrived just after dark chained to four other convicts, and they were assigned cells for the first night. Unable to sleep, he lay on his bunk until around midnight when one of the other convicts started screaming. The cellblock soon became what he referred to as "a chorus of the dead," causing Walker to believe he had mistakenly been assigned to the lunatic asylum instead of the state penitentiary.

But he was, in fact, in the state prison and soon learned that many of the convicts at Huntsville were probably borderline asylum cases. He seems to have adjusted to the rigors of prison life quickly; his nine years in the Galveston County jail probably prepared him well for the penitentiary.

Two years later, in 1885, he was assigned to the wood shop when he watched the young inmate cut off his fingers intentionally in order to return to his wife at home. Despite the success of the inmate's actions—he was pardoned one year later based, in part, on his disability—Walker steadfastly refused to mutilate himself.

He did, however, descend into a period of "hopelessness and despair" and began to question if life as he knew it at Huntsville was worth continuing.

The chance meeting of a former inmate he had known during his years in the Galveston County jail intensified some of those feelings of despair. At Huntsville, Walker came across an acquaintance he identifies only as "an old darkey from Galveston who was a hoodoo practitioner." This particular inmate had been a slave on the plantations of Virginia and had talked with Walker for hours about his slavery experiences before the Civil War.

When the former slave was presented for trial, his "hoo-doo bag" failed him, and he was sentenced to four years at Huntsville. Walker had assumed he had seen the last of the old man when he was shipped from Galveston.

But after he was himself transferred to Huntsville, he recalled, he did see the man again, and it was a traumatic moment for him. "I never saw him again until two years afterwards when they brought him here from some outside camp," Walker recalls. "He was completely worked down and his hair was as white as cotton."

The old man looked like the "living dead," and Walker saw his own future in similar terms. He claims to have helped get the old inmate a relatively easy job in the prison kitchen, where he worked until his discharge and return to Virginia.

Walker, after arriving at Huntsville, was first assigned a job as a messenger in the machine shop. He later was transferred to the blacksmith shop and worked as a striker with a convict doing a fifteen-year sentence for horse theft.

Every morning at a certain hour the other convict would become very agitated and then quickly settle down again. As Walker gained the confidence of his co-worker, he asked him about it one morning, and the inmate pointed towards the west gate at a gray horse. It was the horse he had stolen six years earlier resulting in his fifteen-year sentence, and each morning a prison official would ride up and hitch the horse briefly. As soon as the horse was taken away, the other inmate would become calm again.

Eventually Walker was assigned to the kitchen, considered a preferential assignment and one that indicates he was serving his time without disciplinary problems.

On December 19, 1902, the assistant superintendent called him in to inform him his application for a pardon had finally been granted by the governor.

Twenty-nine years after the murder conviction, the document verified the indicting evidence against Walker had been circumstantial and that prison officials had concluded Walker was right-handed. During Walker's stay at Huntsville, it would later be revealed, prison officials and guards had for twenty years secretly watched him at work attempting to catch him working predominantly with his left hand—something they were never able to accomplish.

On the grounds of the circumstantial evidence and the fact Walker was right-handed, the governor had made the pardon full and unconditional and had restored full citizenship and the right of suffrage.

Like Andrew George a few years earlier, A.J. Walker's claims of innocence were finally verified, and he, too, would be released from prison.

Three days later he was again summoned from his job, lined up with some other inmates, and marched to the prison commissary store where he and the others were issued their "citizen suits of clothes." He was awarded five dollars for nearly twenty years "service to the state" but also to cover transportation expenses back to Galveston County.

He was then released through the gates at Huntsville to return to a society in which it had been nearly thirty years, including his jail time, since he had been a free man. He was escorted to the train station by the prison chaplain; an action that he seemed grateful for.

Back in Galveston, his wife had waited those twenty-nine years for his return, and he was eventually reunited with her and with his now-grown daughter and three grandchildren.

Like many other narratives, *The Life of A.J. Walker, an innocent convict* appears to have been published largely to promote Walker's claims of innocence of the charges against him. But unlike most of the other prison memoirs, his is amazingly free of bitterness towards the prison system. His anger was directed at the courts and not the penitentiary that had incarcerated him.

But despite his positive approach to his prison experience, the terrible set of circumstances that had cost him three decades of his adult life obviously left its mark on Andrew J. Walker. The tone and direction of his conclusion in *The Life of A.J. Walker, an innocent convict* seem to say it best:

> I am kindly welcomed and treated well by all whom I meet, though one can never forget the great wrong that has been done him by perjury through the courts of our country, and can never out live the sting and disgrace which he is forced to undergo. While life lasts the sting will remain.

Chapter Twenty-Seven

What Was a
Bertillion Officer?

Located inside the vaults of the Texas State Library and Archives in Austin are volumes of old, bound ledgers, approximately two feet by three feet closed, containing prison inmate records dating back almost to the very beginning of the prison system in 1849.

Inside these ledgers are the hand-scribed notations on inmates as they were processed into the Texas prison system. On October 5, 1878, a journal entry is posted for Convict #7109. The inmate is listed as having dark hair, hazel eyes, and a light complexion. The physical inspection of his body revealed wounds and scars over virtually every part of his torso—many of them gunshot wounds. This twenty-six-year-old inmate was named John Wesley Hardin.

It would be another decade before Texas prisons attempted to categorize inmates by physical characteristics; in 1878 state officials were only able to document body markings such as scars and tattoos.

Seven years later, in 1885, Andrew George recalled, "Here I was weighed, description taken and pulled off my citizen clothes and put on the stripes of a convict."[1] From his description, it is impossible to tell if George was given the same physical inventory as Wes Hardin or if he was subjected to a new technique in criminal identification—the Bertillion Method.

In Europe, a police clerical officer by the name of Alphonse Bertillion began measuring prisoners in 1883 in an attempt to categorize and identify criminals using aliases. He started measuring jail and prison inmates and recording the length and width of their hands, the length of their fingers and forearms, and their head sizes. His identification system became known as the Bertillion Method, and using this technique, he identified his first recidivist in 1883. In 1884 he correctly identified 241 inmates and was recognized for developing the first scientific method of criminal identification to be used by a police force.

American police and prison officials quickly adopted the Bertillion Method. It is not known if Texas had implemented the system by 1885 when Andrew George was processed into the penitentiary, but in the 1890s Charles Campbell recalled that "They then marched us to the underkeeper's office, where the necklaces were taken off and one at a time we got on the measuring stand and then into the office, where a convict clerk asked a few hundred questions as to age, nationality, occupation, habits and the like."[2] Campbell's description of a "measuring stand" does indicate a Bertillion Method inventory.

J.S. Calvin, in 1898, stated that upon processing, "After breakfast we were marched to the bath house where we were stripped of our citizens clothes and while we were naked we were thoroughly examined to locate all the marks and scars that was on our bodies."[3]

At some point during that period, the Texas prison system did adopt the Bertillion Method, and the officer in charge of making the incoming physical inventories of convicts became known as the Bertillion officer.

The problem that Texas prison officials and other correctional and enforcement officers were encountering was the inability to ensure uniformity in measurement. Different officers frequently obtained different measurements on the same individual, in part due to a lack of agreement on how tightly the calipers should fit in order to obtain the measurement. Another problem involved the natural aging process: As people age, so do many of the bodily characteristics.

In a high-publicity case, the Bertillion Method was eventually discarded as the result of an inmate in the federal prison at Leavenworth, Kansas, being identified as a previous convict. The use of fingerprints, however, proved decisively that the inmate identified by the Bertillion Method was in fact in another prison system at the same time.

This occurred in 1903 and led to the adoption of fingerprinting as the method of identifying physical characteristics of criminals, a technique quickly adopted by the state of Texas.

As for Alphonse Bertillion, he had himself become the first policeman in Europe to solve a murder by use of fingerprints a year before the Leavenworth incident. Bertillion continued this new scientific approach to become a foremost authority on fingerprinting as well as on the use of photography and other police forensics.

But the fingerprinting office at Huntsville continued to be referred to simply as the Bertillion Office. As late as 1925 Milt Good reported that during his processing and after showering, "his next step was to go through the Bertillion Office. Here the prisoner is stripped and a list is made of all identifying marks, fingerprints are taken, and photographs made for purposes of identification."[4]

As identification techniques improved, a Bertillion officer processed virtually every incoming jail prisoner and prison inmate. By the 1930s the Bertillion officer had also become responsible for issuing "wanted" posters for criminals avoiding arrest and for escaped convicts from the jails and prisons.

For nearly a century fingerprinting has been considered a scientifically validated method of identifying criminals. Even more reliable and error-free methods have been developed in recent years, however, including the use of DNA testing and retinal eye scanning by cameras. The position of the Bertillion officer has been replaced by a processing officer who finger-prints, photographs, takes blood samples, and may even use a camera to record blood vessels on eye retinas. The new pro-cessing officer is today a medical-scientific practitioner.

But in Texas prisons, as far back as 1849, some prison offi-cial processed in new convicts in some manner, even if hand-scribing a description of identifying marks in a ledger. By the late-1880s that officer was referred to as the Bertillion officer.

---

1   George, Andrew L., *The Texas Convict: Sketches of the Penitentiary, Convict Farms and Railroads, Together with Poems*, pg. 11.

2   Campbell, Charles C., *Hell Exploded. An Exposition of Barbarous Cruelty and Prison Horrors*, pp. 13-14.

3   Calvin, J.S., *Buried alive, or, A term in the Texas State Prison, 1898-1902: a chapter from real life*, pg. 31.

4   Good, Milt, *Twelve Years in a Texas Prison*, pg. 24

Chapter Twenty-Eight

Breakin' Rocks in the Hot Sun, Texas Style

Breaking rocks in the hot sun has traditionally been associated with chain gangs in the American South. During the convict lease period in Texas, however, prisoners were typically used for other tasks such as fieldwork, lumber camps, and working on railroads.

There was one rock-breaking project, however, and it could have been classified as Texas-sized by any standards. It involved carving large blocks out of a solid granite mountain.

In 1882 Texas found itself rich in undeveloped land but poor in financial capital and in desperate need of a state capitol building to replace the previous structure that had been destroyed by fire.

Austin, still a struggling community trying to establish itself, promoted the building of a grand structure to house the seat of state government. That government, not surprisingly, readily agreed and made plans for a magnificent limestone building to sit at the head of Congress Avenue.

Architectural plans were drawn up and contracts were signed. Some government officials and others were not pleased that the construction contracts were awarded to an out-of-state firm, but at least the building itself would be constructed of native Texas limestone.

The lack of working capital wasn't really a problem; the contractor would be paid in free land located to the northwest in the Panhandle area of the state—literally thousands of acres.

Likewise, the lack of money wouldn't be a problem in recruiting and paying skilled quarrymen to excavate and transport the massive stone blocks necessary for construction. It was thought the state might even make a profit in this venture because it was leasing unskilled state prison convicts to the contractors for a paltry sixty-five cents a day. At that time breaking rocks in the hot sun was considered an appropriate activity for prisoners—it kept them busy and out of trouble.

A readily available source of native limestone was located nearby that would save even more money for the state. Just west of Austin, the Oatmanville quarry had a good supply of stone that would only require a nine-mile rail line. Inmates started building that line immediately and completed the job in March of 1884.

Politicians and citizens alike watched as the railroad was completed and excavations begun on the hill overlooking Congress Avenue. A railhead was constructed at the site of the new capitol building and ten derricks were erected. They were massive cranes with sixty-five-foot masts and fifty-foot booms capable of handling the huge limestone blocks that would soon be arriving from the Oatmanville quarry.

Work had also started at the quarry site, and state convicts were dispatched to learn the quarryman trade through on-the-job training. Working on the limestone outcrops, the inmates began excavating the large stones that would be needed for the foundation of the new capitol building.

The inmates had been dispatched from the state prison unit at Huntsville and were housed in wooden shacks at the quarry site. On November 18, 1884, they started work; eventually up to one hundred convicts would be utilized. Within months they were producing up to ten railroad cars of limestone blocks a day, and progress was moving along in Austin as the blocks were being laid for the foundation of the new building.

Oatmanville would eventually be renamed Oak Hill and is today a subdivision of south Austin. Driving west on Highways 290 and 71, there are limestone outcrops on the left just past where William Cannon Boulevard intersects and before Highway 71 divides off to the northwest.

In those outcrops it is possible to see a large area that has been obviously excavated, and this is where the convicts had begun cutting and removing the limestone blocks from the cliffs.

The work was hard and very dangerous, but the initial blocks were cut on schedule and loaded onto rail cars and transported to the railhead at Congress Avenue.

Those first blocks, however, were so disappointing that the contractor and Texas politicians decided not to use them except for the underground foundation and interior structure of the building. The coloring of the stones was not uniform, and small iron particles in the rock quickly began staining the blocks with rust marks. There were some initial discussions of transporting out-of-state limestone to construct the building, but the overwhelming sentiment was to continue with native stone.

The work at the Oatmanville quarry was short-lived but not without considerable danger. Eight convicts were killed during the excavations and buried in unmarked graves nearby. Five of the prisoners died of disease or abuse, and three were killed attempting to escape. Given the fact that only one hundred inmates were used there, those figures represent a high mortality rate. Today that area is referred to as Convict Hill, and a street bearing that name was later built.

But nine miles to the east, in Austin, the politicians were still trying to find a suitable alternative for the poor-quality limestone. Governor Ireland favored the use of red Texas granite, but the contractor objected to building with the more dense—and therefore heavier and harder to work with—granite.

Finally an unlimited source of free granite blocks was made available near Marble Falls; the contractor agreed to work with the stone, and the decision was made that the exterior of the Texas state capitol was to be constructed of granite rather than limestone.

But the agreement had come at a high cost to the inmates in the prison at Huntsville. The contractor had agreed to the switch to granite only on the condition the state provide up to a thousand more convict laborers to work the new quarry near Burnet and Marble Falls. In a period when skilled quarrymen were earning four dollars a day, the convict laborers would cost only sixty-five cents per day, and that money would be paid to the prison system, not the prisoners who were doing the work.

Existing rail lines could be used to transport the blocks from Burnet to Austin, but a new sixteen-mile track would have to be created from the granite dome, called Granite Mountain, which was near Marble Falls.

The state prisoners completed the sixteen-mile narrow gauge railroad from the granite quarry to Marble Falls in November of 1885, and room and board facilities for the convicts were established at the quarry.

Convict laborers began rough cutting and excavating the huge stones, and mule-drawn flatcars were used to haul the blocks to the dressing and shaping grounds at the quarry. A steam locomotive named, appropriately, the "Lone Star" began what would be a four-year project of transporting 15,700 carloads of granite from the quarry to the building site in Austin

The "Lone Star" locomotive would haul nearly 16,000 carloads of granite from Burnet to the construction site of the new state capitol in Austin.

It would seem Texas had found the perfect solution for the problem of building a world-class capitol building in Austin. But other problems developed quickly. Unions resented the use of convicts to do what they considered a "scab job" and ordered a boycott of the capitol project by all union workers.

The convicts could be used to cut and excavate the blocks, but they had no training or experience in "dressing" the stone and actually constructing a building with it. With unions boycotting the project, the contractor was forced to advertise overseas for skilled stonemasons and obtained the services of eighty-six skilled workers from Scotland. The Scottish cutters arrived at New York only to be met by American union members and a U.S. marshal. Their recruitment, it turned out, was a violation of the Contract Labor Act of 1885.

Eventually they made their way to Austin and began work while the contractor fought the issue in the courts and was eventually assessed a fine. That fine would later be reduced to what basically amounted to a slap on the hand.

On the first anniversary of the granite contract, a "public relations" trip was planned for members of the capitol board and the Texas prison administration. According to the *Austin Statesman*:

> A splendid dinner was served. There are at present 200 convicts engaged in quarrying and 100 in cutting the stone. There are also 148 regularly paid stone-cutters, making 448 men now at work dressing the granite for use here in Austin. The convicts are behaving well. The stone-cutters are perfectly satisfied. The quarries seem to be alive with men. Huge stones are piled up in every direction.[1]

The completed capitol building was opened to the public on April 21, 1888, and dedicated during the week of May 14-19 that year. Texas had pulled off a spectacular land exchange for a beautiful pink granite state capitol building that was unquestionably world class in design and construction. The building is second in size only to the national capitol in Washington, D.C. In 1888 it represented one of the seven largest buildings in the world.

Meanwhile, back at Granite Mountain, the donation of free stone to the state paid off handsomely for the landowner, who later sold his land and the granite dome for $90,000—a fortune in the late 1800s.

The dome, it turned out, contained some of the finest grade red and pink granite in the world. After surveying, it would be determined the dome was also the largest pink granite mountain in the United States, encompassing some two hundred acres in mass.

Over a four-year period, up to a thousand of these Texas prison inmates were used to quarry the granite stone for the capitol building. This photo suggests that some of the prisoners were able to do shaping work on the stone after quarrying.

The sale of Granite Mountain in turn led to the development of a granite quarrying industry in Texas that continues to this day. Texas granite can be found literally around the world in buildings and monuments. More than 225,000 tons of the stone went into the construction of the seven-mile Galveston seawall. And still, more than a century after the quarrying began to obtain the capitol stone, the granite dome appears to be hardly diminished in its supply of pink and red stone.

Inside the new building, structural and ornamental cast-iron was used throughout the interior. From the Rusk penitentiary, inmates at the iron-ore foundry cast fluted columns, ornamental stairway banisters, and other decorative and structural iron pieces that can be seen throughout the capitol building.

This photo of the shaping yard at the Granite Mountain quarry shows the massive size of the stones that inmates were quarrying by hand for the state capitol building.

Mule-drawn carts would haul the raw stone from the Granite Mountain quarry to the shaping and finishing yards near Burnet.

This is the Granite Mountain quarry in Burnet County where up to a thousand leased Texas inmates quarried the huge boulders of rock from the granite bluffs in the top of the picture.

The owner of Granite Mountain, thinking the land worthless, donated this stone for construction of the new state capitol. The use of leased convicts eliminated much of the labor cost for the state. After completion of the capitol, the landowner sold his land at a handsome profit and Granite Mountain would become the cornerstone of a very successful quarrying industry that continues in Texas today.

Leased convicts were closely supervised at the Marble Falls quarry. Note the bloodhounds in the far right side of the picture. These guards and dogs watched over the inmates by day, and by night they patrolled a two-acre fenced compound where the prisoners lived and slept.

These shackled inmates were leased to the contractor quarrying the granite stone for the state capitol building in the mid-1880s. The tight security resulted in few escapes during the project. The inmate in the foreground is a "dawg boy" handling a pack of bloodhounds to assure no prisoners do escape.

TEXAS STATE CAPITOL BUILDING

Perspective
No.1

This is the architect's original plan for the state capitol building to be constructed with limestone. The change to granite required some modifications, but the final structure today is very similar to these plans.

Today the Marble Falls quarry is closed to the public, but it is still possible to visit a roadside picnic area just north of Marble Falls on Ranch-to-Market Road 1431 and, like at the old Oatmanville quarry site in Austin, view part of the quarry and the early railroad tracks.

Few inmates ever got to see the finished masterpiece in Austin, but most experts doubt that the Texas state capitol building could have been built without their leased labor to the contractor who constructed it.

1   *Austin Statesman*, January 31, 1886.

Chapter Twenty-Nine

(1898-1902)

Buried Alive

The Texas Prison Memoir of J.S. Calvin

Then I began to wonder whether the Texas State Prison was a human institution, or whether it was something like the old Spanish inquisition that I had read about in history. I have read of the horrors of the penal institutions of Europe and Rome, and the abuses and starvation of the English and Russian penal colonies and of the tortures of ancient and Eastern prisons...But my dear friends, after my experience with the Texas State prison I have come to the conclusions that all that you or I have read about the horrors and tortures of ancient prisons might be applied to the Texas State prison without exaggeration.

Shortly after midnight on July 5, 1898, a mule-drawn wagon loaded with newly convicted prisoners worked its way through the darkness to Rusk penitentiary from Jacksonville, Texas, where the inmates and their guard had missed the last train connection to the prison.

As the shackled men sat uncomfortably on the wagon bed in the hot Texas summer air with a bright moon above, they approached the prison around one o'clock in the morning.

That first view of the dreaded prison was later recalled by one of the men, a convicted counterfeiter:

> The country about Rusk is hilly and when we came in sight of the walls we were on a high hill, apparently way above the walls, and as the moon was shining bright we could see the walls, the coal ovens, and the pipe foundry, and they seemed to me to cover more than a hundred acres of ground, and reminded me of a vast cemetery.

The association of Rusk penitentiary with death would be a theme that the inmate making that observation, J.S. Calvin, would later use to describe his experiences in the Texas prison system. That narrative, appropriately, was titled *Buried alive, or, A term in the Texas State Prison 1898-1902.*

J.S. Calvin was a New Englander who had left his Boston home to travel to Texas in the hopes of making money. Calvin, however, didn't do it the old-fashioned way; he literally made money by printing it.

Since counterfeiting was a federal crime in the 1800s, it is not clear why Calvin was sentenced to a Texas prison rather than a federal penitentiary, and Calvin doesn't go into detail about his conviction.

But he was clearly sentenced by the judge and jury to a term of hard labor in Texas, and his first impression of Rusk penitentiary on that summer night could not have prepared him for what he was about to endure inside the walls.

J.S. Calvin was about to experience the Texas convict lease system firsthand; he would, during his relatively short four-year term, experience the brutality and terror of being leased to work in brickyards, iron mines, wood crews, and finally, on the infamous railroad squads.

Buried Alive represents one of the most graphic accounts written during the convict lease period in Texas, and in it Calvin paints a brutal picture of the conditions under which Texas prisoners were forced to live and work while earning the state of Texas about one dollar a day for their labor.

While still at county jail with a new eight-year prison sentence ahead of him, Calvin describes the despair of being notified that the prison transfer agent had arrived to take them to Rusk.

On July 4, 1898, he and the other prisoners were ordered out of their cells and lined up two abreast; white inmates in one line and black prisoners in the other. Then they were "necked," or chained together with metal bands around their necks and connected to each other about two feet apart on long chains.

The actual transfer from the jail to the train station was a humiliating experience that Calvin refers to several times in *Buried Alive*. He recalls that the inmates were paraded through the streets of the town like exotic circus animals, providing a show for the local townspeople.

Since it was the Fourth of July holiday, the town was packed for the annual parade and festivities. The sight of chained and manacled prisoners being marched through the streets only added to the general merriment of the crowd and the humiliation of the prisoners.

When the train was thirty minutes late, the prisoners were forced to stand on the platform, shackled and chained, while the local citizens gathered around laughing, making jokes, and jeering at them.

Throughout the day, as their train stopped at various stations, other crowds would gather and also taunt them. During the long trip they were never fed and were forced to change train cars three times, causing them to miss their last connection at Jacksonville. Because of the late hour, they were transferred to mule-drawn wagons and hauled the approximately seventeen miles to Rusk in the darkness.

A counterfeiter, Calvin did not consider himself a hardened or violent criminal, but he quickly found that his conviction did not protect him from being housed and worked with many convicts who were.

His naiveté is apparent from the beginning of *Buried Alive* as he arrives at the darkened gates of Rusk penitentiary. Surprised at the number of armed guards who greeted them at the prison unit, he relates, "I had supposed that when we got there we would get to go to bed and rest for the night but they marched us through a long hall and around into another large building and there proceeded to line us up and search us."

Then, after complaining about traveling all day in the July sun without food, they were given a big pan full of cold, boiled fat bacon and cold, burned corn bread.

He was then shown a cell and with three other convicts, told to sleep on a blanket spread on the stone floor—something he was unable to do. After a few hours, a gong sounded and the general inmate population got up for work.

After the other inmates had eaten, Calvin and the other new arrivals were removed from their cells and given some more fat bacon, cold black coffee, and rice with black molasses.

They were then stripped, their bodies inventoried for tattoos and scars, issued their prison uniforms, and assigned a permanent two-man cell that he described as "barren," with a double bunk six feet by three feet and packed with a straw mattress.

Although he had not slept for nearly two days and had eaten almost nothing during that period, he was assigned to work in the brickyard that first day. The guards told him that, being a new convict, he wouldn't be expected to do a first class day's work until he had gotten "seasoned."

"I began to think then that it was not so horrible an institution as I had first supposed," he writes in another indication of his naiveté. This supposition would not last long, and within a few pages *Buried Alive* begins using references to the Texas prison system in terms such as "horror," "terror," "torture," and "Spanish Inquisition."

He worked the remainder of that week on the brickyard and on Sunday was allowed his first weekly bath and shave. On that day he received the dreaded news he was being transferred to the Woodlawn state farm, seven miles outside Rusk, to work the fields.

Upon arriving at Woodlawn, he learned the living and working conditions were far more primitive. He quickly became friends with an inmate working as a doctor and used that friendship to receive a hospitalization order and exemption from outside fieldwork.

His efforts to beat the system, however, were short-lived when he was transferred back to Rusk after three weeks so an able-bodied inmate could replace him at Woodlawn.

Thinking he had outsmarted the prison officials and escaped the dreaded work crews, Calvin was then shocked to learn he had been assigned to the iron mines working the ore beds. It was there he truly began learning of the "horrors of the institution."

Still new to the system, he writes that in the beginning he almost dreaded Sundays—the only day when inmates were not required to work. "When I was not at work the time seemed to drag by with a monotony that made a week seem like a year," he writes.

But like the seasoned veteran convicts in Texas prisons in the 1890s, he would quickly learn the value of any time off from the work crews. On August 24, 1898, he was transferred to a location known as "Camp Rice."

His attempts to avoid work by feigning illness did not work here, he reports. At Camp Rice, prison authorities referred to a "sick inmate" as one who collapsed and died on the job. Everybody else was considered healthy enough to work.

Calvin claims he had been legitimately sick while assigned at Rusk and that after reaching Camp Rice, his claims of illness fell on deaf ears. He was immediately marched nearly four miles to the work site and assigned the task of chopping one and one-quarter cords of wood. When he complained of being sick and unable to work, the guard told him: "The hell you can't—God damned your old lazy soul, you don't know that you are in the penitentiary. You get up from there and go to work or I'll strap you!"

After a period of adjustment at Camp Rice, Calvin was told he and the other inmates were being leased to the Texas Midland Railroad to clear and lay track to run from Garrett to Greenville in Hunt County.

After being neck-chained and transferred to Terrell, they were again met by a large crowd of townspeople who had gathered to observe and taunt them. They were then marched to the prison boxcars that would transfer them to the worksite.

"When we entered the cars we found them just like a bake oven. They had stood there all day in the hot sun." Forty-five convicts were crowded into each car, given some fat bacon and corn bread, and told to go to sleep. Calvin and the others would quickly learn that these boxcars were to be their "dormitories" at the worksite.

The following day was a Sunday, and they were transported in their "cells" to an area some twenty-two miles south, where they would begin clearing land for tracks.

Calvin, by this time, must have earned a level of trust with the prison officials because he was given a position as a convict foreman in charge of the work crews. As such, he is able to provide, in *Buried Alive*, a rare view of the administration of the convict lease system through a prisoner's eyes.

He soon realized that as a convict foreman, he would not be able to satisfy the demands of the railroad officials. The Texas Midland Railroad was paying the state of Texas ninety cents a day for each inmate laborer, and when a railroad official complained to the head prison guard about the lack of work progress and threatened to cancel the labor contract, the result was even more brutal conditions for the convict laborers.

"Hell! I can do more work with 25 convicts than you could do with 100 free laborers," Calvin reports the prison guard responded, and the immediate result was even harsher work conditions and hours.

It is during this period Calvin began to equate the Texas prison system with the Spanish Inquisition, Roman enslavement, Russian penal colonies, and Eastern prisons.

His period of naiveté was clearly over.

He claims their prison guard had previously worked a gang of lifer Negroes until they were almost dead. In desperation the inmates had finally "bucked," or refused to work anymore. As a result the guard was threatened with termination and then assigned to the Texas Midland Railroad job. On this job, Calvin alleges, the officer had been given the ultimatum that another "buck" would result in his being fired.

The newly assigned guard arrived determined that every inmate would produce his quota of work and no convict would ever refuse to work.

Despite their inhuman conditions they made incredible work progress, but the railroad officials continued to complain. The guard, fearing termination, responded by reporting that Calvin and the other prisoners were "lazy" and requested permission from Rusk administrators to "get them right."

Permission was granted.

Calvin reports the prison officer ordered the men together one morning and produced a leather strap three inches wide and eighteen inches long and attached to a wooden handle. It was the instrument usually referred to as the bat.

Picking out an inmate, apparently at random, the guard then instructed that prisoner to remove his pants and lie on the floor. Four other inmates were ordered to grab his hands and feet and hold him face downward while thirty strokes of the leather strap were administered. The inmate writhed in agony and cried out in "piteous yells and groans" until the punishment was finished. Then another three inmates were given the same treatment.

With a warning that four convicts would be strapped each day until they increased their work production, they were then sent back to the fields. Already stretched to the limit, the inmates somehow found a way to work even harder, but Calvin reports the guard continued to strap two or three men every month just to keep them scared. Calvin was to remain on this work squad for three years.

During that period, the late 1890s, various reports of the brutal treatment of convicts, and even rumors of the murder of inmates working under the convict lease system, were surfacing throughout East Texas.

Calvin reports that:

> My friends it is not my intention to give you an account of all the details of all the deaths that occurred under my observation but to give you an account of only a few of those that were most impressive to me for they are buried from Howland in Lamar County to Ennis in Ellis County and in some places, two in a place. They are buried on the right of way of the Rail Road, just as we used to bury a cow. Except that they

were buried in a suit of stripes and a cheap pine coffin; but with just about as much formality and sympathy as a lot of old paddays usually manifest while burying a cow. And during the last days on earth of a person dying in prison he is attended only by his fellow prisoners and they are in no position to minister to him for all of them that are able have to work all day and at night they are not able to render much service to the sick.

He relates a story about a fellow inmate who fell beneath a train car and crushed his leg. Forced to lie in the hot sun all day without medical treatment except chloroform administered by an inmate doctor, he died before being returned back to the camp with the rest of the work squad that evening. Calvin resolved that if he lived through his sentence, he would somehow one day make the incident known to the rest of the world.

The following year, during a dry, hot summer, the work squad suffered terribly from heat exhaustion and typhoid fever. But despite the illness and misery, the work schedule was increased and the guard would yell, "Come on with them shovels, come on with them shovels, God damn you lazy devils; the state has got to get you right and take in this train."

When the rate of deaths had become so high the prison system couldn't send enough replacements, an official from Rusk visited the site and ordered the guard to stop whipping the prisoners. After the official had returned to the main unit, however, the inmates were then submitted to other forms of punishment.

"A poor ignorant Mexican who couldn't speak English was chained so he could stand only on one foot and kept there until midnight" in one case. Other punishments included being wrapped in chains in the summer sun and being hung by chains for hours in the doors of the boxcars.

This torture continued until September of 1901, when a new guard was assigned to the work squad and they were transferred to another location to lay a sidetrack for a cotton platform. The new sergeant was more considerate of the conditions of the inmates and treated them better, with the result that within ten days the crews were hardly working and had begun fighting among each other.

Calvin reports the only repercussion was that two inmates were given three licks apiece with a black strap much smaller than the hated bat. The other inmates, seeing this as a sign of weakness on the part of the guard, continued to slack off and fight with each other. Finally, out of desperation, the new officer singled out the problem makers and administered twenty-five lashes to each of them with the bat.

Order was restored without interruption for the next nine months. During this period they were again transferred—this time to a contract farm in Hunt County, along the Sabine River. With order and discipline restored and working conditions under the new sergeant greatly improved, Calvin reports his remaining time was relatively humane.

Governor Lanham pardoned him in 1903, a little over four years through his eight-year sentence. He left prison, in his words, a living skeleton of a man.

Buried Alive gives us a rare detailed account of the daily existence of inmates assigned to work squads during the convict lease system, especially on those state leases involving the railroads. The title, in itself, indicates the depth and intensity of J.S. Calvin's personal experience.

Buried alive, or, A term in the Texas State Prison, 1898-1902: a chapter from real life was printed in Paris, Texas, in 1905. In his introduction, J.S. Calvin makes some general observations about the laws of Texas and the criminal justice system in general. In prison, he states, there are three classes of men: victims of "vile" persecution or evil circumstances (in other words innocent men who were "railroaded"), men influenced by evildoers who actually violated laws, and hardened criminals living life through an "installment plan" at the penitentiaries.

He does not really tell us just exactly where he feels he fits into this criminal formula. *Buried Alive*, however, presents a very graphic description of the horrors he encountered in prison, and he is consistent in his objection that, as a counterfeiter, he should not have been incarcerated with the more violent and hardened criminals he was forced to live with for nearly five years.

Chapter Thirty

Eating What a Dog Would Spurn

Inmates, like soldiers, are notorious for complaining about their food. This is as true today as it was in 1885 when Andrew George complained about his first prison meal at Huntsville: "We sat down to eat with knife and fork, tin plates and tin cups. The breakfast consisted of sour corn bread cooked the evening before, boiled bacon and black coffee. Though I was hungry and had no supper the day before, I could not eat this breakfast."[1]

Since food was so important to the inmates, especially in the convict lease years, almost every narrative written afterward refers to the food—or the lack of decent meals. Their narratives provide an idea of what Texas convicts were fed from 1875 to 1925 at the Rusk and Huntsville prisons, on the state farms, in the woodcutting camps, and on the cotton plantations.

Henry Tomlin, writing about the food at Rusk in 1889, also described the regimented procedure inmates were expected to follow when eating:

> At the tap of a triangle (a big piece of steel in the shape of a V, suspended by a wire, that is used in giving orders) we marched each man with his right hand on the shoulder of the man in front of him. We

marched to within about three steps of the dining room door and halted; then at another tap of the triangle we entered the dining room. Here we were shown our respective seats by a "flunky" who managed to wedge in four or five to the bench and then we stood until the gong sounded again for us to sit down; and each man then made a grab for his plate and fork to get ready for eating. I will have to explain something of the eating regulations, which are very strict. The soup is served to each man to start on, and if a man wants more he merely holds up his pan, as none are allowed to speak above a whisper. If one wants bread, he holds up his knife; if meat, he holds up his fork, and for vegetables he holds up his plate, and his cup for water. If one should lack any of these or should want anything; he must hold up his hand closed. Then a waiter comes and he whispers the request, and the waiter either gives it to you or reports to the steward, and if he does not order it for you, you do without.

After we had finished eating, the knives, forks and spoons were piled upon the end of the tables and a "flunky" stood ready, with large cans, to collect them. At a given signal from the steward these "flunkies" make a dash to rake them off into the cans, which makes considerable din. Then they make a dash to the kitchen and deposit their load. The steward taps the triangle and the convicts arise from the table, form in line and are marched out in the same order that they came in, each man with his right hand on the file leader's shoulder, until out to the dividing walk, where they break ranks and each man starts to his allotted place of work....[2]

The rule of silence was strictly enforced during dining—at Huntsville and at Rusk—in the 1800s. Here, Charles Favor illustrates a scene in which an inmate steward is carrying food to the inmates. Notice the two inmates with their hands raised—an elaborate system of hand signals indicated what an inmate wanted since speaking was not allowed. Favor, Charles A., *Twenty-Two Months in the Texas Penitentiary* (Corsicana, TX: Democrat Print, 1900).

This regimented eating procedure must have been in effect throughout the prisons in Texas because John Shotwell described almost identical procedures at Rusk only six years later: "Our meals in the dining room were served in rusty tin plates, and we made signs for what we wanted to eat. If we wanted meat we would raise our fork, or for bread, raise the knife. When noon came, we would take a seat on the ground, forming a circle, and one of the convicts would serve us with dinner, which consisted of spoiled bacon, boiled corn and stale corn bread."[3]

Later, as a convict leased to a cotton plantation near Cameron, Texas, he recalled: "We were fed on spoiled hog-head, stale corn bread and coffee made of burned corn bread crust."[4]

Bill Mills, initially assigned to the Burleson and John Farm in 1910, suggests the eating procedures had changed little since Henry Tomlin's 1889 description and Andrew George's complaint of the food itself:

> The guard told us to line up in front of each other with our right hands on the next man's right shoulder. He and the picket guard counted us into the dining room where there was a long table about three feet wide. We sat down on each side, facing each other. There was one waiter they called a "flunkey." He passed the food around to us, as it was not served on the table in family style. The prison rules were more strict then than they are now. The prisoners were not allowed to speak a word in the dining room. We used signs instead of speaking. For instance, when we wanted bread, we would hold up a knife, and for meat we would hold up a fork; for salt we knocked on the table with our knuckles; for syrup we closed our fists and stuck our thumbs up horizontally; but if it was vinegar we wanted, which was served in quart bottles on the table, we would make the same sign except the thumb would be straight down. They served coffee once, for breakfast only, so that when we sat down to breakfast those who wanted water would turn their cups down and those who wanted coffee left them up. If we wanted something served in our plates we held the plate up.
>
> For breakfast, as a rule, we would get biscuits, but many mornings we would have cornbread. We would have syrup, and flour gravy....

Our menu for dinner consisted of cornbread, one piece of boiled meat, and peas most every meal— sometimes turnip greens. This was usually the meal the year round except when they gathered Irish potatoes in the spring and sweet potatoes in the fall. Our supper menu was exactly the same as dinner. [5]

Nor did the food seem to get any better with the end of the convict lease system. In 1921, nearly a decade after the "official" end of the leasing of convicts in Texas, Beecher Deason was assigned to a woodcutter's squad outside the Huntsville unit and recalled, "I looked up and saw a trusty coming in a wagon. He had our dinner. He put a bunch of tin plates in two rows about six feet apart on the ground, and put spoons in them... Two or three men were chosen by the head flunky or waiter or the boy that brought our dinner to help dish out the dinner. It was in cans ranging in size from five to twenty gallons, and consisted of beans or peas, bacon, corn bread and sorghum molasses."[6]

During the convict lease system period and the years immediately afterward, it appears the prison cooks could not have functioned without the staples of hog meat and corn bread.

The combination even assumed its own slang. When the field workers weren't producing enough work, they would be told by the boss: "You gonna miss that ol' hog and bread tonight."

But of all the narratives, John Shotwell, in *Fourteen Years in Hell*, seemed to describe it best: "Not until you have lived in rotting rags, eating what a dog would almost spurn...."

1   George, Andrew L., *The Texas Convict: Sketches of the Penitentiary, Convict Farms and Railroads, Together with Poems*, pg. 11.

2   Tomlin, Henry, *Henry Tomlin, the man who fought the brutality and oppression of the ring in the state of Texas for eighteen years and won. The story of how men traffic in the liberties and lives of their fellow men*, pp. 24-25.

3   Shotwell, John, *A Victim of Revenge or Fourteen Years in Hell*, pg. 11.

4   Ibid., pg. 17.

5   Mills, Bill, *25 Years Behind Prison Bars*, pp. 8-9.

6   Deason, Beecher, *Seven Years in Texas Prisons*, pp. 2-3.

Chapter Thirty-One

(1892-1894)

Twenty-Two Months in the Texas Penitentiary

The Texas Prison Memoir of Charles A. Favor

Then the "building tender" showed me a bed where I should sleep. It was on the bottom tier. I bunked with another man. His clothing was damp with perspiration; he had an odor about him that was not pleasant; the bed smelled from want of air, but I crowded in, and, notwithstanding the hardness of my bed, I fell asleep. How long I slept I do not know, but when I awakened I had not rested. I thought to raise up and allow some of my muscles to relax which had contracted from the cramped position in which I was sleeping, but when I did so the guard yelled "lay down there old white man!" I did not know but that he might shoot the next minute so down I went and there I lay until I was certain I would provoke no further censure from that vigilant gentleman.

Charles A. Favor was born two years after the Civil War, in 1867. His German father and Missouri pioneer mother moved to Cooke County, Texas, in 1869. In 1892, when he was twenty-five years old, he entered the Texas prison system at Rusk.

His account of his prison experience, which he published in 1900, was titled *Twenty-Two Months in the Texas Penitentiary*. In it he claims he had had a relatively good childhood and normal young adult life prior to being sentenced for swindling in Navarro County.

As a child, he reports, he was given a good education but "turned out" at age thirteen. While he doesn't explain what "turned out" meant—orphaned or sent off to school—his education must have been substantial because he was employed as a teacher in the Navarro County public schools at age seventeen. On July 20, 1886, he was married in Purdon, Texas, and in 1892 he was convicted of swindling and sentenced to prison.

Because of his education and teaching background, Favor provides an excellent and descriptive account of convict life and working conditions at Rusk penitentiary. *Twenty-Two Months in the Texas Penitentiary* also contains a number of crudely drawn sketches that offer some illustration to his story. He doesn't indicate if the drawings are his work or the contributions of someone else, therefore their accuracy is suspect.

Favor arrived at Rusk penitentiary after being transferred from the Corsicana jail. He and several other prisoners were chained by their necks and marched in pairs to the train station to be met by the prison transfer agent. In Tyler, they stopped to pick up some more prisoners, and to Favor's chagrin they were chained to some black prisoners and left in a train car overnight.

The next day they arrived at Rusk and were forced to strip and scrub themselves before being shorn and shaven. Despite the lack of sleep from the boxcar experience the night before,

Charles Favor offers this illustration of Texas inmates in the late 1890s. This was a period when striped uniforms were used in Texas. Favor, Charles A., *Twenty-Two Months in the Texas Penitentiary* (Corsicana, TX: Democrat Print, 1900).

they were sent to the fields that same day to work on iron ore crews.

There, on one of the slag piles, he was ordered to dig, screen, and load iron ore without gloves, resulting in his hands immediately becoming raw and bloody. When he complained to the guard nearby, the answer was: "That is d—n bad."

Somehow, despite his fatigue and lack of sleep, he made it through that first day and then was forced to run three miles back to the main prison unit that evening. When he arrived he states he was "ready to die." Not sure if he could withstand the physical demands of convict labor crews, he asked himself, "Is life worth the living?" He was, after all, a teacher by trade and not conditioned for the physical labor demanded at Rusk.

On his first night in prison, he was forced to share a filthy, stinking mattress-less wooden bunk with another convict. In less than twenty-four hours at Rusk, Charles Favor had learned why the Texas prison system had such a terrible reputation.

But he was able to adapt to the physical regimen of the work crew, and for ten days he worked in the ore beds before being sent to a coal camp. There, he joined an eight-man work crew cutting ten cords of wood each day to fire the boilers in the smelter. Since he was new and inexperienced, he was required to spend much of his time holding the maul while another inmate swung a sledge. Almost immediately he had a finger cut off.

Favor learned quickly, kept out of trouble, and was assigned a preferential inmate job as a clerk.

In that capacity he was removed from the rigors of the work crews but placed in a position to observe the administration of criminal justice in Texas prisons through the eyes of an inmate bookkeeper. His sentence was relatively short, and he spent much of it in what would have been considered easy work assignments, yet he dictates his memoir with the experience and background knowledge from those weeks he had spent on the ore and wood crews. Given his educational background and writing ability, he provides a unique and probably accurate view of the convict lease years in Texas at the close of the nineteenth century.

Twenty-Two Months in the Texas Penitentiary describes the various methods of punishment Favor observed while in prison. In one passage he relates his own experience of being disciplined in the dark cell where he was forced to lie naked on the rock floor with an old, filthy quilt. In total darkness and sweltering heat, he was soon sweating and suffering the bites of unseen insects. "I never was so tormented in my life," he later recalled.

Like all of the other prison narratives of that period, Favor describes the use of the bat to punish inmates. He describes his first experience being forced to watch another inmate strapped and the dread of watching him strip and lay down on the floor before begging in wild, child-like screams for mercy.

Later he would be assigned to a bunk located near the whipping area, and he witnessed many more beatings—the most brutal of which was a convict lashed on his stomach and then his back until he passed out. Revived with water, Favor alleges, the inmate was then strapped again.

Over the months, he recalls, some men would beg, cry, promise, grunt, and scream while others would struggle not to make a sound. "It is said that it requires a man with a nerve next akin to madness to count the licks as they are applied," he writes, suggesting that some inmates actually were able to do so.

Favor makes a bizarre suggestion that strapping be replaced in Texas prisons with what he envisioned as a "slapping machine." This machine, he suggests, would be a bottomless chair with paddles attached underneath, operated with a system of springs. The springs could be given so much force per square inch to the paddle and a mounted register would record the number of strokes administered. With this documentation, he felt, the officers would no longer be able to abuse the thirty-nine-stroke limit per inmate and would not be able to lash the convicts in overly brutal strokes.

"Many states are now making great strides along the line of Prison Reform," he writes, "and may grand old Texas occupy a leading place among the states in this movement."

Unfortunately, strapping would continue in Texas prisons for another half century. One hundred years after *Twenty-Two Months in the Texas Penitentiary* was published, many critics continue to argue in the courts that Texas is still lagging in prison reform.

Favor makes other observations about the prison system, including the use of bloodhounds for maintaining work crews and chasing escapees. Although he doesn't indicate he was ever transferred from Rusk to Huntsville, he also makes some general but apparently accurate observations about the physical plant at that prison.

Twenty-Two Months in the Texas Penitentiary describes what prison administrators in the 1800s called "crank's row." During that period, the term "crank" was used to identify prisoners with mental problems, and "crank's row" was an area set aside, usually maximum security, to segregate these prisoners from the general inmate population.

Favor, however, suggests that often prison officials would throw a normal convict into the "crank's row" as a technique to discipline him. Many reports of that period, including official penitentiary audit papers, record that the treatment of mentally ill inmates bordered on sadistic torture. Favor recalls one ex-convict who told him of being thrown into a "crank cell" as punishment and forced to stand, chained to the bars, twelve hours a day for two months.

According to *Twenty-Two Months in the Texas Penitentiary*, the inmate was forced to stand against the bars with his hands chained above his head. The inmate recalled endless hours of listening to the criminally insane wail, cry, and scream as they were chained beside him. After two months he was removed from the bars, strapped, and shackled with a ball and chain riveted to his leg.

This story would be impossible to verify, and Favor presents it as what it was, an ex-convict's account. Unfortunately too many other accounts, including official state versions, verify that this treatment was common in Texas prisons in the 1800s.

Favor makes several other observations about life at Rusk prison including one issue several other writers also complained about during the convict lease years—the poor condition of, or complete lack of, brogan shoes for the inmates.

"Up to the time of my leaving," Favor claims, "there had never been a man received that those shoes would fit. I have often thought that the lasts upon which they were made must have been made by some tribe of prehistoric times. You can easily determine if a man is an ex-convict by taking off his shoes. So hard and ill-fitting are convict shoes that they wear off all the toe-nails."

Charles A. Favor was a relatively well educated man who served time in Texas prisons during a period of much alleged and recorded brutality. He worked on the iron ore squads and woodcutting crews briefly before becoming a bookkeeper, but those experiences, coupled with his ability to write, give us a very descriptive account of prison life in the 1890s.

Twenty-Two Months in the Texas Penitentiary is also notable in that many of the reform suggestions Favor made in the 1890s, the "slapping machine" being a notable exception, would eventually be legislated and incorporated into Texas correctional guidelines, although many of them would require a century to implement.

Chapter Thirty-Two

Huntsville's "Dummy"

During the period 1875 to 1925, it was common for judges, when sentencing convicted criminals to prison, to use the expression "sentenced to 'hard labor' in the state penitentiary..."

And, especially during the years of the convict lease system, "hard labor" meant just that. Many of these narratives suggest that upon the day of arrival, the inmates were quickly processed and assigned to work squads that very same day.

Some jobs, the sought-after positions, required some degree of skill and knowledge. Leatherworkers, tailors, wheelwrights, blacksmiths, and other prison jobs were given to convicts with previous skills in those areas and whose disciplinary records were acceptable to prison officials.

However many jobs, especially those at the lease camps, required only a strong back—chopping or sawing wood, picking cotton, and shoveling coal. A keen or dull mind was irrelevant.

The initial assignment to a job, menial or skilled, relied in large part upon the inmate's responses during the preliminary interview and processing into the prison unit.

At the Huntsville unit, the interior of the prison was divided into two yards. The lower yard was the industrial sector of the prison unit and usually referred to by the inmates and guards as simply the "lower yard." But in prison, nearly everything assumes a name of its own, and the lower yard quickly became known as the "dummy."

This early 1900s photograph shows the lower yard of the Huntsville unit—known as the "dummy." Photo by Gary Brown, courtesy of the Texas Prison Museum

In 1921 Beecher Deason wrote, "We were sent down to a place they called the 'dummy' (why it was called this I never knew) and put to shoveling coal."[1]

But Bill Mills, who had arrived at Huntsville a decade earlier, in 1910, explained, "When new prisoners arrived and had changed garments, they would be put to work the first few days on the dummy. The dummy was a place on the lower yard near the boiler room where the prisoners would saw wood to fit different stoves to sell to prison guards and officials and to furnish heat for all the prisoners. The reason for calling it the dummy was because one could work at it regardless of intelligence."[2]

So the dummy came to represent not just the lower yard at Huntsville, but also the assignment of any menial task within that yard whether it was shoveling coal or cutting wood. In 1921 another inmate (not Deason) also reported that he was first put to work on "the dummy," a job of unloading coal at Huntsville.[3]

One of the last references to the dummy during this period was by Milt Good in 1925 when he recalled, "I was next sent to the lower yard, known as the 'Dummy.' The newcomers work here until they are assigned to a regular work within the walls or transferred to a prison farm. At six o'clock a.m. all men not assigned to jobs report to the West Gate and some are placed on the 'Wood Squad' and taken in trucks to the forests to cut cord wood. Those who remain are checked in to the foreman of the 'Dummy' for the day."[4]

It appears then that by 1925, the dummy had become a staging area within the Huntsville unit for inmates who would be assigned duties—in effect somewhat of a "utility squad." Today in Texas prisons, utility squads are work crews of inmates, usually older prisoners or those with physical limitations, who do a reduced work load at various odd jobs around the unit.

From 1875 to 1925, however, utility workers in the dummy were not doing reduced workloads at odd jobs. Back then the "dummy" represented the "hard labor" that the judge had ordered.

1   Deason, Beecher, *Seven Years in Texas Prisons,* pg. 2.
2   Mills, Bill, *25 Years Behind Prison Bars,* pg. 26.
3   *It's Hell in a Texas Pen, the barbarous conditions as told by ex-convicts and unearthed by the Legislature,* pg. 21.
4   Good, Milt, *Twelve Years in a Texas Prison,* pp. 24-25.

Chapter Thirty-Three

Texas State Railroad

From the very beginning of the convict lease system, the railroads were the industry with the closest ties to the program. The association of Texas railroads with nearly free convict labor actually started in 1867 immediately after the conclusion of the Civil War and would continue until the abolishment of the system in 1912.

By 1896, nearly thirty years after the first railroad contract with the state, Texas decided to get into the railroading business itself. The project would become known as the Texas State Railroad and would continue until 1909 after thirty-two and a half miles of track had been established. But in another sense it continues yet today as the Texas State Railroad State Historical Park.

The influence of the Texas prison system is evident throughout the East Texas area around Palestine and Rusk; numerous prison units are located in or around those two communities today.

But the convict lease system was most closely identified with the old prison unit located in Rusk. The Fourteenth Legislature authorized the prison in 1875, and at a time when the entire prison system was basically leased out to the firm of Cunningham and Ellis, the penitentiary was built to relieve overcrowding at Huntsville. Construction took place from 1877 to 1883.

The location at Rusk was also designed to take advantage of the iron-ore deposits in East Texas, and a smelter known as the "Old Alcalde" was built in 1884.

By 1896 the smelter and the Texas venture into iron-ore production were proving unprofitable and difficult to sustain because of logistics problems in obtaining the ore and transporting it to the smelter as well as other problems such as the processing of wood into charcoal to fire the furnace.

Labor wasn't a problem; the state had a seemingly endless supply of inmates to send to the sawmill camps and coal mines. While sawmills such as the one at Alto, near Rusk, had atrocious reputations as work camps, it was in the mines that the "work 'em to death" philosophy prevailed. When one convict died on the job, he was literally dragged out and replaced with another.

By the mid-1890s the transient sawmill camps and mines were unable to provide the necessary wood and coal for the furnace at Rusk mainly because of the problems in transporting the materials by mule and wagon through the East Texas forests. The decision was made to build a railroad—a state railroad.

In 1896 inmates started clearing land and laying rail from the iron foundry in the northern part of Rusk westward across Bean's Creek into the piney woods. Logistics efficiency (but not financial profit) was increased, and in 1903 the smelter was expanded. This required more raw materials, so the railroad was extended another five miles and a smaller prison unit known as Camp Wright was established.

Camp Wright was a woodcutting camp located nine miles west of Rusk in the midst of scattered homesteaders isolated deep in the East Texas piney woods. Inmates assigned to the camp were required to cut at least a cord of wood a day and sometimes as much as a cord and a half depending on the supervisor. The wood would then be processed as charcoal for the furnaces at the main prison unit.

By 1906 Camp Wright began attracting civilians living in the area who were looking for employment, and a small community developed. The location, however, was known simply as Camp Wright and consisted of temporary wooden barracks housing leased convicts.

Still the venture was failing to show profit, and Governor Thomas M. Campbell convinced the Texas legislature to operate the railroad as a common carrier and to extend the line from Camp Wright to Palestine in 1907.

This would stimulate the growth of civilians around Camp Wright, and by 1910 speculators began actively developing a township. Because Governor Campbell was closely identified with the initiation and growth of the Texas State Railroad, it was decided to name the community after his daughter.

At the town's inauguration, the community's namesake, Maydelle Campbell, participated in the ceremonies and the township became known as Maydelle, Texas. Always directly related to the Texas State Railroad, Maydelle continues to exist as a community today.

Although the Texas State Railroad was successful in providing raw materials to the smelter at Rusk, the continuing loss of state revenues was problematic. Governor Campbell's decision to extend the line to Palestine was designed in part to expand the supply sources for the iron smelter but almost certainly also to develop passenger service.

At Rusk, the St. Louis Southwestern Railway Company of Texas and the Texas and New Orleans Railroad Company both had rail connections, and to the west in Palestine, the International and Great Northern Railway Company was an established route. A state-owned rail connection between these two towns and the three railroads would open a potentially profitable rail passenger connection.

But the project would require a twenty-two-and-a-half-mile extension through difficult East Texas terrain consisting of pine forest, underbrush so thick a man could hardly lift his feet to walk at times, wild animals, snakes, mosquitoes, and poisonous vines. In the summer months the heat and humidity would be unbearable, and the winter months could bring blue northers with bone-chilling winds and near-freezing temperatures.

Finding skilled men willing to work in these conditions clearing land and laying track would have been cost prohibitive. The answer again was the convict lease system, and inmate crews set to work immediately.

Chopping their way through pine, dogwood, oak, hickory, and willow trees covered with trumpet creeper, they cleared land and laid rail westward. Crossing the Brigman Branch, they continued to Talles Creek and built a bridge spanning over 700 feet.

Just past that bridge, at the confluence of Talles Creek and One Arm Creek, the prison system had established a coal mine to supply the Rusk furnace. That mine, in turn, had spurred the development of a small community including a sawmill, several stores, and a post office. The post office required that the community adopt a name, and around that time, according to local lore, a community dance was held in which a girl allegedly "lost" her petticoat. The undergarment was later found, supposedly, and had been fashioned from an old coffee sack with the word "Java" imprinted on it. The new community, if the story is true, was thus named Java, Texas, and thrived during the period that the mine and railroad construction were in the vicinity.

The convict lease crews continued westward, and Java would eventually all but disappear with most of the local citizens moving to Maydelle.

The crews continued to clear brush, cut ties, lay rail, and move towards Palestine at an inhuman pace. Beatings and lashings were commonplace and occurred daily. Several of the narratives during this period report the daily arrivals at Rusk of inmates who had been killed or maimed working on the project. Others returned to Rusk without fingers, hands, or toes—victims of self-mutilation to escape the crews. There was never a problem replacing them with new prisoners.

Fourteen miles out of Rusk, a sawmill was established north of the tracks to supply lumber, much of it in the form of railroad ties. Named for a member of the state prison board, the work site was known as the Mewshaw State Sawmill.

Here, the prison system built a sawmill and rustic housing for the prisoners assigned there and the guards who supervised them. At one point a cog rail was extended two miles from the camp to facilitate the transport of logs to the mill. The Texas prison system would continue to use the site until Rusk Penitentiary closed in 1917 although the mill had burned down in 1912. Today the site is vacant—marked only by a state historical marker along Highway 84.

From the sawmill, the tracks continued west to the Neches River near the Ben Cannon Ferry. Established in 1848, the crossing was at that time a toll bridge and would continue in operation until 1924.

At the Neches River crossing, the convict crews constructed a wooden bridge spanning 1,100 feet and supporting locomotives and rail cars some thirty-five feet above the riverbed. Local lore claims that the civil engineer who designed the bridge also rode the first locomotive to cross it. According to the legend, the wooden structure shook so badly that the engineer felt the bridge was about to collapse and jumped from the train to his death. The bridge didn't collapse but today has been replaced by a concrete structure.

The crews continued toward Palestine across the Sumac Branch of Stills Creek and the community of Jarvis just ten miles from their destination at Palestine. Jarvis may have gotten a temporary boost from the nearby construction of the Texas State Railroad but eventually disappeared.

The Texas State Railroad ran from Rusk to Maydelle and was later extended to Palestine. Convict lease crews built the line and the Mewshaw sawmill camp utilized inmates to cut, mill, and deliver lumber for various railroad operations in the area.
Photo by Gary Brown

By now the convict crews were living off the railroad themselves. Sometimes they would sleep nights chained inside railcars, even in the brutal summer months. Other times the supervisors would simply force them to sleep in holes in the ground, sometimes covered by logs and brush but often just open to the elements. During rainy periods they worked and slept in the mud.

Clothing was almost never replaced, much less laundered. Bathing and clothes washing occurred when the rail line crossed a creek, which was irregular at best.

From Jarvis, the terrain became especially difficult with underbrush making progress literally measured in feet per day. At times the land turned into swamps, forcing the crews to work up to their waists in water for days at a time. Many of the prisoners had worn out their state-issued brogan shoes and were working barefoot at this point.

Throughout the rail line, but especially along this stretch before entering Palestine, rumors and newspaper accounts claim that the tracks were lined with the unmarked graves of convicts killed trying to escape or simply worked to death.

Fighting snakes, many of them poisonous, and working at times with burlap bags over their heads to avoid the black swarms of mosquitoes in these swampy areas, the inmate crews finally forced the steel tracks through to Palestine in 1909. In all, some thirty-two and a half miles of track had been extended from Rusk to Palestine. Depots were created at Palestine, Maydelle, and Rusk, and passenger service was started on April 15, 1909. The Maydelle to Palestine rail extension had cost Texas approximately $530,000.

The governor and the prison commission of the state of Texas operated the Texas State Railroad. The convict labor that had been used to build the line had been described by the press and later convict narratives as particularly cruel working conditions with extremely high numbers of often-unreported deaths of the workers.

Initially prison crews staffed the trains supervised by a civilian engineer. The foundry at Rusk closed in 1913, and Rusk Penitentiary itself was closed four years later. As a transporter of raw materials for the iron-ore smelters of the prison system, the Texas State Railroad was no longer needed.

As a connecting line for the railroads operating out of Rusk and Palestine, however, the state line was able to show some profit through its passenger service. Prison crews were replaced with civilian staff.

The year before the Rusk Penitentiary closed, 1916, the railroad owned two locomotives, thirty-seven freight cars, and two passenger cars and actually showed a slim profit from passenger and freight revenues.

However, by 1921 the railroad had run up a deficit, was leased to the Texas and New Orleans Railroad, and was used as a freight carrier with some passenger service.

By 1962 the Texas and New Orleans Railroad had been purchased by Southern Pacific, which cancelled the lease with the state. Attempts were made to lease the tracks to the Texas South-Eastern Railroad Company and the Missouri Pacific Railroad Company, but both leases were generally unsuccessful.

In 1970 the Cherokee and Southwestern Tourist Railroad Corporation attempted a tourist attraction on part of the route without success, and by 1972 the abandoned tracks were donated to the Texas Parks and Wildlife Department. Plans were developed to tear up the tracks and make the right-of-way into a hiking and bicycle trail between the two towns.

Significant public interest, however, indicated that there might still be a market for a vintage railroad line operated as a state park, and the Texas State Railroad State Historical Park was created.

From 1972 to 1976 a second group of inmate workers was brought in to clear brush, replace ties and rail, and shore up bridges. This time work conditions were vastly improved. Inmates worked ten-hour days, were fed well, and were transported to the nearby Eastham and Ellis prison units nightly.

On America's bicentennial, July 4, 1976, the state park opened with tourist passenger service between Rusk and Palestine again in operation. Steam locomotives built from 1901 to 1927 were found, refurbished, and placed into service along with a considerable number of coaches, tank cars, boxcars, and other rolling stock—cars dating back to the 1910s and completely refurbished and operational again.

Almost immediately the Texas State Railroad became a favorite with film producers, and the state park facilities and equipment have been used for numerous movies, documentaries, and television programs.

In 1996 inmates from the Texas prison system were used again to work on the tracks, marking over a century of connection between the railroad and the prison system. Inmate crews spent some 16,000 hours in community service between 1996 and 1998 working not only to maintain the railroad tracks but also restoring passenger coaches and assisting with the rebuilding of a steam engine.

Today the Texas State Railroad State Historical Park is transporting a new generation of Texas children and their parents between Palestine and Rusk again, a tradition over a century old. The steam trains cross thirty bridges in the East Texas countryside and cover fifty miles on their round trips between the two towns. Along the route automobiles stop at crossings and people stand outside to wave as the locomotive engineers use their steam whistles in return.

It is possible to get a "feel" for train travel as it must have been in the early 1900s in Texas. It is also possible to drive between Rusk and Palestine on Highway 84 along the north side of the tracks and stop at Maydelle, the Java Crossing, the site of the Mewshaw State Sawmill, the Neches River, and other spots.

It is a fun experience for all ages, and in many ways the system could be called the jewel of today's Texas state park system.

But it wasn't fun for the unfortunate convicts picked to work on the project in the late 1800s. And along the tracks today it is impossible, from the restored passenger cars, to really imagine what they endured.

The Texas State Railroad, built during the convict lease period of the late 1800s, is today open to the public and operational as the Texas State Railroad Historical Park and provides steam locomotive passenger service between Palestine and Rusk, Texas. Photo by Gary Brown

Gone today are any reminders of their plight: wild animals, snakes, mosquitoes, and poisonous vines. The misery of heat, humidity, and even blue northers is lost when viewed from a padded seat in a 1914 Pullman passenger car. Today's passengers riding in trains moving at 25 miles per hour do not suffer the terrible mosquito swarms that the original inmate

This 1911 photograph of a steam locomotive on the Texas State Railroad was taken a year before the convict lease system was "officially" abandoned in East Texas. Photo source: Texas State Archives

Inmate "engineer" on one of the Texas State Railroad steam locomotives. Photo source: Texas State Archives

crews had to work in and suffer with through nights spent sleeping in muddy holes.

The Deanwright Crossing and Beaver Pond areas outside Palestine are scenic and serene viewed from the train cars but once required convicts to slosh through snake-infested water ankle-deep for days at a time—often barefoot—while pounding bridge supports into the East Texas mud. And gone too are the graves too numerous to recall, and unmarked anyway, of the inmates who died building this railroad line.

The condition of these prisoners was one of the more sordid aspects of one of the most shameful episodes in Texas history. That the fruits of their labor and misery would today provide enjoyment and memories for thousands of children and adults is both ironic and somehow fitting. The Texas State Railroad State Historical Park is in some ways a lasting memorial to what they created more than a century earlier.

It's just a shame the inmates themselves are hardly remembered.

Chapter Thirty-Four

(1925-1935)

Twelve Years in a
Texas Prison

The Texas Prison Memoir of Milt Good

One day in the dining hall a convict discovered a small lizard, thoroughly stewed in the turnip greens. He held the lizard up by its tail and called the steward. When the steward came and examined the lizard he said: "Where did you find that?" "In my turnip greens," replied the convict. Steward: "How long have you been here?" Convict: "About two years." Steward: "That's not long enough to entitle you to a whole lizard. Give half of it to somebody else."

$\mathbf{M}$ost convicted felons arriving at Huntsville for processing into the Texas prison system were relatively unknown outside their counties of conviction.

Occasionally an inmate whose trial had been prominently covered in Texas newspapers, such as A.J. Walker from Galveston County, would arrive and the guards and prison administrators would recognize him from the notoriety.

But for the most part, the frightened and dispirited inmates who arrived for processing into prison were just nameless faces. They were also men who all looked surprisingly similar after they had been shaved and issued prison uniforms.

But on January 24, 1925, one of the inmates arriving at Huntsville was very well known and making it apparent that he didn't consider himself a "typical convict." His behavior and demeanor indicated he expected some special considerations.

Not surprisingly, he also continued to proclaim his innocence.

That new inmate, Milt Good, came from a well-known, respected, and successful Texas family that traced its roots back to the homesteading days in Caldwell County during the 1840s.

But Good's reputation and notoriety that January morning in 1925 was not based upon his ancestral history. What had preceded him that day was the newspaper coverage, throughout Texas, of his conviction for killing two inspectors for the powerful, wealthy, and influential Texas Southwestern Cattle Raisers Association.

Milt Good would serve ten years in the Texas prison system and later publish a narrative of his time titled *Twelve Years in a Texas Prison by Milt Good, As told to W.E. Lockhart*. Much of the early part of his narrative is a documentation of his family history and the events leading up to the charges of murder against him.

Good does, however, include a later description of his years locked up, 1925 to 1935 (he includes two years in jail awaiting trial), and *Twelve Years in a Texas Prison* provides a good description of Texas prisons in transition.

Of all the narratives in *Texas Gulag*, Good's account, despite being blatantly self-promoting, describes the Texas prison system during the transition period from state-owned farms into the reform-oriented administrative years under the management of Lee Simmons. It was during Good's decade in prison that Texas finally succeeded in abolishing chain gangs.

In *Twelve Years in a Texas Prison*, Milt Good claims a "reasonable education" and a positive childhood. He covers, in considerable detail, his personal history including early work on cattle ranches, his marriage, financial disasters in 1917 and 1918, and his attempt to earn a living as a rodeo cowboy beginning in 1919—an endeavor he claims resulted in his being declared the world champion steer roper in 1920.

Then in 1923 his troubles changed his life completely. Good is vague about the actual events leading up to the "trouble" but writes that on a Sunday evening in March of that year a shooting took place near Seminole, Texas. When the trouble was over, two inspectors for the Texas Southwestern Cattle Raisers Association were dead. Good and a partner were arrested for murder.

Good claimed both of the Association inspectors had records as killers and dangerous men and he and his partner "could have run away from this trouble, but we had both been raised in the West and had not been taught to run from anything or anybody."

Law enforcement authorities, however, contended that the night before the District Court was to convene to investigate evidence on cattle stealing, the local judge, district attorney, and two Texas Southwestern Cattle Raisers Association inspectors were meeting at the local hotel. Good and his co-defendant, they later claimed, burst into the meeting and shot down the two witnesses against them in cold blood.

Good surrendered and was placed in jail without bond. On April 1, 1923, he was charged with two counts of murder. In June a Lubbock jury sentenced him to twenty-six years in prison for the first killing. Three months later an Abilene jury added another twenty-five years for the second death.

The sentences were then "stacked," meaning the second sentence started *after* the completion of the first. From a legal standpoint, this meant Milt Good had fifty-one years to serve in the Texas penitentiary.

Good appealed and remained in county jails for another year and a half until his appeals were denied. Then Bud Russell arrived and escorted him to the Huntsville prison unit on January 24, 1925, and he was processed into the prison system as Texas Inmate #52153.

At that time not all convicted criminals were sent directly to Huntsville. The practice was to transfer all state prisoners to Houston and then ship them out to the various prison units as needed. Milt Good was assigned to the main unit in Huntsville, generally considered the most favorable assignment since many of the state-operated farms still had brutal and terrible reputations carried over from the convict lease system years.

From Houston he was transported with seven other prisoners and received his first experience with "the chain." Attached to another prisoner with a chain locked around his neck, Good was then connected to a larger group of prisoners by a longer chain. Thus shackled, he was forced to keep step with the other convicts to keep from choking himself as they moved about.

At Huntsville he was stripped, issued a prison uniform, and given a physical examination that included a blood test for social diseases. After the examination, he was classified as fit for hard labor and sent to the Bertillion Office for a profile card.

The processing described in *Twelve Years in a Texas Prison* is the first narrative to suggest Texas was beginning to implement a scientific approach to recording and classifying prisoners. It also indicates just how much Texas prisons had changed from the 1870s, when John Wesley Hardin's processing had consisted of a hand-scribed description in a large ledger, to Good's 1925 examination including blood sampling.

Good admits he had a relatively easy assignment at the Huntsville prison compared to the conditions of inmates assigned to the farms. On the prison farms, he reports, the inmates worked from "can to can't"—the time of day they *can* see until they *can't*.

On his first day he was sent to the lower yard, or dummy, to perform odd jobs. He was then assigned to the guard's dining hall briefly, a job considered by inmates to be a preferential assignment because of access to better food. There, however, Good complained that the "heat from the ranges was killing," and in a progression of job changes, each resulting in better and better assignments, Good was transferred to the creamery. Later he was assigned to the hospital, considered one of the best inmate jobs in prison, at the request of one of the Texas prison commissioners.

Throughout *Twelve Years in a Texas Prison*, Good avoids stating that he was somehow receiving preferential treatment, however the succession of his work assignments and the name dropping he used throughout his memoir suggest he may have been using outside contacts, at least in the early years, to obtain preferential work and living conditions at Huntsville.

But he could not completely avoid the difficulties of prison life, and even the assignment to the prison hospital had its unpleasant duties. Good was given responsibility of taking charge of the bodies of condemned men after they had been electrocuted in the death chamber. He would place them on a "cooling table" in a small room and claims, "I could never get the left leg straightened out. It would be so cramped that it was impossible to straighten it. I think the surgeons or embalmers cut the tendons in the left leg before they could place it straight."

The decade of the 1920s was one of widespread criticism of the state prison system—criticism that was often led by Governor Miriam Ferguson. By the 1930s Lee Simmons would be appointed general manager of the prison system and assigned the job of rooting out corruption and implementing a reform-based approach to corrections in Texas.

This 1930s photograph indicates prison work conditions had improved little since the time of most of these narratives. Notice the spoked wagon wheels against the building—one of the trades taught inmates involved wheelwright work. From John Wesley Hardin in the 1870s to Milt Good in the 1930s, inmates reported being assigned to the wheel shop. Photo source: Texas State Archives, courtesy of Jester III unit, Texas Department of Criminal Justice.

One of the most persistent complaints, Simmons soon found, was that of inmates with money being able to secure favorable treatment and living conditions in prison by "buying" their way through their sentences.

Milt Good, at that time, participated in an action that assured he would have future problems with Lee Simmons and the other prison officials at Huntsville. If Good was, in fact, receiving favorable treatment prior to Simmons' appointment, he ended his special inmate status the night he and several other inmates jumped a guard, beat and disarmed him, and escaped over the walls of the Huntsville unit.

In recounting his escape, Good reveals the attitude that seemed to pervade his entire narrative in *Twelve Years in a Texas Prison*. "We had spent so much money and felt sadly mistreated," he complained.

The escape was followed by a seven-month journey across the West to the Canadian border and back south, ending only when Good was rearrested at Antlers, Oklahoma.

Again Bud Russell arrived to take him into custody and return him to Huntsville. Good continues to complain bitterly of his conviction for the two murders, which he refers to as "prosecution and persecution," and the subsequent efforts of the Texas Southwestern Cattle Raisers Association to assist in his recapture by distributing wanted posters.

He also complains of the persistent efforts of Texas Ranger captain Frank Hamer to apprehend him and suggests that his "personal reputation" was responsible for the well-known ranger being assigned to his case.

Possibly the main reason Frank Hamer did not recapture Milt Good was the fact he couldn't legally cross the state line into Oklahoma in pursuit. Only a few short years after Good's escape, however, Hamer would be assigned another job to recapture two Texas fugitives—a job that would end across the state line of Louisiana with the bullet-riddled bodies of Clyde Barrow and Bonnie Parker.

Good may not have realized it in *Twelve Years in a Texas Prison*, but he was probably very lucky that Bud Russell, and not Frank Hamer, caught up with him in Antlers, Oklahoma.

Throughout *Twelve Years in a Texas Prison*, Milt Good maintains the position that he is the victim rather than the perpetrator. Prison and law enforcement officials, however, did not agree. Back in the custody of angry prison officials after his escape, Milt Good began to learn the true meaning of "mistreated."

At the request of a prison commissioner (Good doesn't relate if it was the same commissioner who had earlier obtained his prison hospital job for him), he claims he was assigned to the wood squad, definitely not a preferential job, and whipped for mugging the guard in the escape attempt.

Good claims the Texas prison system, even with use of the bat, was unable to break him. He claims to have physically warned off a Negro building tender named "Gorilla" and states he took the flogging without being held down. This claim in itself is almost certainly an exaggeration since building tenders kept their positions only through physical intimidation of other inmates, and to have backed down against Good would have resulted in "Gorilla" losing his highly sought after job.

After the sixteenth and final blow, Good reports, the warden asked him if he'd had enough. He claims he told the warden, "You are putting it on; satisfy yourself," and that he then told them they were a bunch of heathens and fifty years behind times.

If this account is true—and there should be very serious doubt that it is—Milt Good was certainly one of the toughest inmates to ever do time in Texas prisons. Virtually every account of the administration of the bat, and there were many accounts, suggest that it effectively broke even the baddest of the tough inmates in the fields and inside the prison walls at Huntsville and Rusk.

After his whipping, Good records he was assigned for a year to the construction department making wagon wheels, a skill he found potentially useful given his ranching background. Then (and he doesn't explain how he obtained it) he was assigned to the highly desired job of acting as inmate jailer handling county prisoners.

In October of 1927 he was caught in a second escape attempt. This time, working with Charlie Frazier, an inmate with a long history of prison escapes, Milt Good was captured in a tunnel digging under the prison walls.

He was placed in solitary confinement and, he claims, robbed of $235 by the assistant warden. Inmates did not (and do not today) receive pay for working while in prison, and Texas prison policy at that time strictly limited an inmate to no more than two dollars in their possession.

Good's claim of losing $235 to the assistant warden is an admission that he was violating the rules with regards to having money in his possession, a fact that bolsters the impression that he was paying his way through prison.

Lee Simmons, head of the prison system in the latter years of Good's incarceration, recalled in his own memoirs, "Good had turned in another $140 that he had obtained in some illegal manner. He said he knew that prisoners were allowed to have no more than $2 on their persons."[1]

This fact indicates Good was aware of the regulations, and his charge of being robbed by the warden in prison was another attempt to manipulate his way through the prison system.

Good claims he was either in solitary confinement or restricted to his cell, almost without break, from 1929 until 1931. Referring to "Nigger Day," which was actually June 19th (Emancipation Day in Texas), he writes that that date in 1931 was "the day things began to break right for me."

By 1932 Milt Good had been promoted to the position of personal chauffeur for Lee Simmons. Despite his setbacks, he always managed to rise back to the top of the inmate job hierarchy inside the Huntsville prison walls.

Then on December 6, 1932, he received a pardon. Actually, it was a ninety-day furlough issued by Governor

Sterling, and the incoming governor, Miriam A. Ferguson, would extend it for another ninety days.

When Good returned from this second extension on June 5, 1933, he was assigned the job of handling officer and inmate mail at the prison. Given the importance of legal correspondence between lawyers and inmates, this gave Good immense control and influence over the other inmates.

Governor Ferguson, whose own administration was beset with charges of corruption and the "selling" of pardons, finally did issue Good a pardon that resulted in his final release from prison effective January 20, 1935.

Much of what Good recorded in *Twelve Years in a Texas Prison* is suspect because of his unabashed self-promotion throughout the book. The book was released the same year he was pardoned and released from prison, 1935—almost as if he was anticipating his release and was prepared to present his side of his story as he started life as an ex-convict.

Twelve Years in a Texas Prison concludes with Good making some observations concerning the positive points of the prison system; observations on the moral conditions in prison, suggestions for improvement of the state penitentiary system, and a purported copy of his prison conduct record.

This section of *Twelve Years in a Texas Prison* lists several items of questionable content.

"I feel I am largely responsible for the Texas prison rodeos," he claims at one point. Lee Simmons, who is generally credited with implementing the prison rodeo as one of the centerpieces of his reform agenda, admits "Milt helped me organize the first prison rodeo," but the general manager stops short of validating Good's claim of responsibility.[2] Good even offers a photo of himself in white clothing, with a black bowtie, new cowboy boots, and a cowboy hat and captions the picture: "Milt Good dressed for the first prison rodeo which he organized and managed."

His observations in the section titled "Moral Conditions in Prison" give some indication as to why Good might have had adjustment problems with other prisoners while at Huntsville despite his always being assigned favorable jobs:

> The men who form the bulk of the prison inmates come from a rather low moral atmosphere. Of course there are some cultured and brainy men who break into prison occasionally, but the rule is that a rather low class comes here.

"The Mexican prisoners will do anything to secure Marihuana [*sic*] which the Mexicans call 'The Weed,'" he continues. With regards to the black inmates, he observed: "I think it is impossible to keep Negroes from shooting craps. That is just as natural with them as breathing."

Twelve Years in a Texas Prison provides a different view in that it is not written from the perspective of an inmate serving time under particularly difficult circumstances. Despite Milt Good's relatively easy decade behind the walls at Huntsville, his insistence that his first escape from prison was justified because he felt "sadly mistreated" typifies his self-serving approach to this prison narrative.

---

1   Simmons, Lee, *Assignment Huntsville* (Austin: The University of Texas Press, 1957), pg. 194.
2   Ibid.

Epilogue

In January of 1874 a huge celebration was held on the Texas capitol grounds in Austin. Highlighting a day of festivities, a 102-gun salute was given to recognize the incoming governor, Richard Coke, who had just assumed office after a tumultuous and often violent election campaign.

Governor Coke was a Democrat, and his assumption of the office of governor was widely seen as an end to Republican rule in Texas state politics. More importantly, most Texans saw it as the end of Reconstruction.

What Governor Coke actually inherited was a former Confederate state with seemingly insurmountable financial problems and a multitude of social and political problems.

One of those problems was the state prison system, only twenty-five years old but in poor repair and badly overcrowded. The Fourteenth Legislature offered an immediate solution a year later when it authorized the construction of a second prison unit at Rusk.

By 1877 it was decided to simply lease the whole state agency to private interests—literally lock, stock, and barrel. From that period until 1912, Texas would try different approaches to the convict lease program, but the results would never be profitable or acceptable.

The new penitentiary at Rusk, selected to use convict labor to develop the iron-ore industries in that part of Texas, never really was profitable, and the lease programs brought continuous charges of cruel and inhumane treatment of the inmates they were supervising.

Rusk penitentiary, built between 1877 and 1883, was the second prison unit built in Texas. A product of the convict lease system, it was connected closely to the iron industry in East Texas. Never successful financially, it was closed as a prison in 1917 and converted to an insane asylum. Today the prison system again operates it as a state hospital for mentally ill inmates.
Photo by Gary Brown

One result of the attempts to develop the pig iron manufacturing potential of East Texas was the development of the Texas State Railroad from 1896 to 1909. It, too, was a failure financially.

While the Thirteenth Amendment, adopted immediately after the conclusion of the Civil War, was designed to abolish slavery and involuntary servitude, many former Confederate states designed a legal substitute for slavery—"hard labor" as punishment for crime.

Texas would join that movement, and the programs at Rusk and with the Texas State Railroad would be direct consequences of that decision. The program was the "convict lease system" and represents one of the most shameful episodes in this state's history.

It would eventually be replaced after 1912 by a state program of purchasing land and employing convict labor on "state farms," as opposed to leasing them to private interests. Most inmates simply felt they had been given a new overseer to administer the same conditions. It would not really be until the 1930s that significant changes would take place in Texas prisons. The convict leasing system was merely transformed.

The role of individuals such as the Reverend Jake Hodges and news reporter George Waverly Briggs cannot be overstated in leading the crusade to abolish the convict lease system in Texas. Other individuals, notably several courageous members of the Texas legislature, also played key roles in the development of the 1910 legislative report that called for the end of the program.

But the real truth is that the convict lease system in Texas was not abolished out of social or moral considerations. It was abolished because it was unprofitable.

Rusk and the Texas State Railroad were never profitable, and the Depression of 1907 resulted in the collapse of the pig iron market and virtually spelled the end to both the prison unit and railroad.

But more importantly, by 1912 Texas could afford to sustain its own prison system without financial assistance from private industry.

A decade earlier the discovery of oil at a field near Beaumont, called Spindletop, would lead to vast revenues for the state and end the need for Texas prisons to subsidize themselves.

By the time of the "state farms" after 1912, the impetus would be on the prison system attempting to become self-sufficient and self-sustaining—an approach that would be adhered to until the 1980s.

But that period after Reconstruction, roughly 1875 to 1925, would be the most violent, brutal, tumultuous, corrupt, and exciting period in Texas prison history.

It was the period of the Texas Gulag, or the chain gang years.

Bibliography

Inmate Narratives

Calvin, J. S. *Buried alive, or, A term in the Texas State Prison, 1898-1902: a chapter from real life*. Paris, TX. No publisher listed, 1905.

Campbell, Charles C. *Hell Exploded. An Exposition of Barbarous Cruelty and Prison Horrors*. Austin, TX. No publisher or date listed but copyright applied for by the author in 1900.

Deason, Beecher. *Seven Years in Texas Prisons*. No publisher or date listed.

Evans, Max. *Long John Dunn of Taos, From Texas Outlaw to New Mexico Hero*. Santa Fe, NM, Clear Light Publishers, 1959.

Favor, Charles A. *Twenty-Two Months in the Texas Penitentiary*. Corsicana, TX, Democrat Print, 1900.

George, Andrew L. *The Texas Convict: Sketches of the Penitentiary, Convict Farms and Railroads, Together with Poems*. No publisher listed, 1895.

Good, Milt (as told to W.E. Lockhart). *Twelve Years in a Texas Prison*. Amarillo, TX, Russell Stationery Company, 1935.

Hardin, John Wesley. *The Life of John Wesley Hardin As Written by Himself*. Seguin, TX. Smith and Moore, 1896. Reprinted in 1961 by the University of Oklahoma Press.

Hennessy, T.D. *The life of A.J. Walker, an innocent convict: romantic, reads like fiction: real true life....* Iola, TX, Iola Enterprise Print, 1903?

It's Hell in a Texas Pen, the barbarous conditions as told by ex-convicts and unearthed by the Legislature. Dallas?, 1925?, pamphlet on file at the Center for American History, University of Texas at Austin.

King, Edward and J. Wells Champney. *Texas: 1874*. Houston, Cordovan Press, 1974, extracted from *The Great South*: Glasgow: Blackie and Son, 1875.

Mills, Bill. *25 Years Behind Prison Bars*. Emory, TX. No publisher listed, 1939?

Sample, Albert Race. *Racehoss, Big Emma's Boy*. New York, Ballantine Books, 1984.

Shotwell, John. *A Victim of Revenge or Fourteen Years in Hell*. San Antonio, E.J. Jackson Co., 1909.

Simmons, Lee. *Assignment Huntsville*. Austin: The University of Texas Press, 1957.

Tomlin, Henry. *Henry Tomlin, the man who fought the brutality and oppression of the ring in the state of Texas for eighteen years and won. The story of how men traffic in the liberties and lives of their fellow men*. Dallas, Johnston Printing and Advertising Co., 1906.

Walker, Donald R. *Penology for Profit, A History of the Texas Prison System 1867-1912*. College Station, Texas A&M University Press, 1988.

Wilkinson, J.L. *The Trans-Cedar lynching and the Texas Penitentiary; being a plain account of the lynching and the circumstances leading up to it, also a presentation of conditions as they exist in our state penitentiaries*. Dallas, Johnston Printing and Advertising Co., No date given.

Interview

8/15/01—Robert H. Russell Jr. interview regarding his great-grandfather, Bud Russell, the prison transfer agent from 1908 until 1944.

Newspaper Articles

Austin Statesman, January 31, 1886
Houston Chronicle, September 28, 1999

Houston Post-Dispatch, February 11, 1925

San Antonio Express, December 6, 1908

San Antonio Express, December 13, 1908

San Antonio Express, December 20, 1908

San Antonio Express, December 27, 1908

San Antonio Express, January 3, 1909

San Antonio Express, January 10, 1909

Prison Audit Documents

Report of the Inspector, office of the Inspector, Texas State Penitentiary, Huntsville Texas, January 31, 1876.

Report of the Penitentiary Investigating Committee including All Exhibits and Testimony Taken by the Committee, Published by Order of the House of Representatives, August 1910.

Index

160-161, 163-164, 171, 177,
185, 210, 226, 229, 242, 266

N

Negro inmates, viii-ix, 36,
46-47, 51, 57-59, 67, 79, 84,
86, 156, 158, 184-185, 206,
226, 230, 242, 270, 273

O

Oatmanville Quarry, 214-215,
223
One-Way Wagon, 90-93

P

Pistol Pete, (Captain), 143, 145
plantation field leases, v-viii, ix,
1, 8, 11, 14, 21, 23-24, 29,
45, 55-59, 84, 88, 94,
99,108, 118-120, 126,
130-133, 136, 138-146, 166,
172, 183, 187-191, 213, 228,
231, 235, 237-239, 243
punishment, 151-159
ball and chain, 29,
72-73, 102-103,
151-152, 246
bat, vii, 34-42, 73, 117,
122, 128, 138-139,
141, 143, 151, 158,
167, 231, 233, 244,
270
carpenter horse, 156,
186
committing depraved
acts, 158
dark cell, 44, 46, 50-51,
53, 70, 72-73, 117,
120, 134-135, 157,
244

hanging by chains,
152-155
hanging on a ladder,
156
spur, 29-30, 155-156
standing on the barrel,
157

R

railroad leases, v, vii-viii, 12,
17, 79, 82-85, 88, 126-127,
130, 172, 213-216, 223, 225,
229-233, 251-262, 276-277
Houston & Texas
Central Railroad
Company, 12,
126-127
Texas Midland Railroad,
229-230
Texas State Railroad,
17, 79, 82, 251-262,
276-277
Ramsey Unit, 191
Reconstruction, vii-viii, 67, 83,
102-103, 204, 274, 277
religious services, 76, 106, 123,
172-175, 189, 276
Robertson Farm, 97
Russell, Bud, ix, xi-xii, 62,
90-93, 93n, 133, 266, 269

S

Satanta, Chief, 83-89
sawmill camps, v, viii, 2, 20, 29,
126, 130, 172, 184, 252,
254-256, 259
self-mutilation, 1, 8, 11, 94,
112, 168, 201, 205, 255
Shotwell, John, 1-20, 37, 81,
95, 98, 100, 126-129, 196,
237, 239